Workflows That Work

Optimizing Business Procedures:
Proven Strategies for Success and Career Advancement

Workflows That Work – Optimizing Business Procedures: Proven Strategies for Success and Career Advancement

Copyright © 2024 by Angel Marqués
All rights reserved.

No part of this book may be reproduced, stored in a retrieval system, or transmitted in any form or by any means—electronic, mechanical, photocopying, recording, or otherwise—without prior written permission from the author, except in the case of brief quotations for book reviews or similar purposes permitted by copyright law.

This is a work of non-fiction. All content and interpretations herein are based on research and analysis by the author. Any resemblance to real persons, living or dead, is purely coincidental.

Published by Angel Marqués Sánchez
ISBN: **9798302547798**

Hello! I would greatly appreciate it if you could share your opinion by leaving a review on Amazon. Reviews not only help other readers discover the book, but they're also essential for supporting future projects.

If you have a few minutes, please visit the review page by scanning the QR code below.

THE HISTORY AND EVOLUTION OF STANDARDIZATION 5
   The rise of international standards 11
   Lessons from early successes and failures in standardization 19

THE HIDDEN BENEFITS OF WELL-DEFINED PROCESSES 28
   How procedures ensure compliance and mitigate risk in regulated industries 34
   Bridging the gap between strategic goals and daily execution. 45

MAKING PROCEDURES WORK FOR YOU 55
   Best practices for developing work processes 64
   Tools and technologies that support procedural excellence 72

THE ROLE OF COMMUNICATION AND COLLABORATION 82
   Using Communication to Align Diverse Stakeholders in Multinational or Cross-Functional Settings 92
   How Freelancers and Small Teams Can Implement 'Big Company' Standards on a Manageable Scale 104

CONTINUOUS IMPROVEMENT AND INNOVATION 118
   The role of feedback loops in refining processes 132
   Case studies of organizations that transformed through procedural innovation 145

BECOMING A PROCEDURAL CHAMPION 159
   Skills and mindsets needed to drive change and foster collaboration 170
   Turning procedures into a personal and organizational advantage 185

DISCOVER MORE 198

The History and Evolution of Standardization

Before the rise of structured work procedures, the industrial world was marked by inefficiency, unpredictability, and inconsistency. Factories operated under a patchwork of methods, often relying on the personal intuition and varying skills of individual workers. This lack of standardization resulted in products of uneven quality, slow production rates, and frequent mismanagement of resources. The industrial revolution had laid the groundwork for mass production, but it lacked the cohesive systems necessary to fully harness the potential of machinery and labor. Employers and workers alike navigated a chaotic environment where the absence of clear processes often led to wasted effort and missed opportunities for growth.

The challenges were most apparent in manufacturing, where the demand for goods was steadily rising. Without standardized approaches, factory floors were often sites of trial-and-error, with workers left to interpret tasks in their own ways. Supervisors, too, had limited tools for ensuring consistency, relying heavily on verbal instructions and oversight. This fragmented approach not only hampered productivity but also made it nearly impossible for companies to scale operations effectively. Growth often brought logistical nightmares, as attempts to replicate success across multiple sites were thwarted by the lack of uniform methods.

Workers in this era faced immense challenges, as the absence of formal training or clear job descriptions left them struggling to meet fluctuating expectations. Tasks were frequently assigned based on perceived skill rather than systematic evaluation, leading to confusion and inefficiency. While the rise of mechanization offered new possibilities, it also underscored the need for coordination between human labor and machine operation. Factories were equipped with powerful tools, yet they lacked the procedural frameworks needed to unlock their full potential. The disconnect between available technology and human organization became an increasingly evident bottleneck.

Moreover, the lack of standardization created an unpredictable work environment that fostered dissatisfaction and instability. Inconsistent workloads, vague expectations, and poorly defined processes contributed to high turnover rates and strained labor relations. Employers struggled to maintain order, often resorting to arbitrary rules and disciplinary measures that did little to address the root causes of inefficiency. The absence of clear processes not only hurt productivity but also eroded trust between management and workers, creating an atmosphere of mutual frustration.

It was against this backdrop of disarray that the seeds of modern work procedures were sown. Visionaries like Frederick Taylor and Henry Ford emerged as transformative figures, determined to impose order on the chaos of industrial production. Their efforts were not merely about improving efficiency; they represented a fundamental shift in how work was conceptualized and executed. By recognizing the limitations of the existing system, these pioneers laid the groundwork for a new era, one in which procedures would become the cornerstone of organizational success. The chaotic industrial landscape of the late 19th and early 20th centuries was not merely a challenge—it was the catalyst for innovation that would redefine the nature of work itself.

FREDERICK TAYLOR: THE FATHER OF SCIENTIFIC MANAGEMENT

Frederick Winslow Taylor emerged as a pivotal figure in the transformation of industrial work at the turn of the 20th century. Often referred to as the father of scientific management, Taylor sought to replace the disorganized, intuition-driven methods of his time with a systematic approach rooted in analysis and precision. In an era where inefficiency was rampant, his ideas provided a framework for maximizing productivity and minimizing waste. Taylor's philosophy rested on a belief that work could be studied and optimized through a series of deliberate steps, creating a standard for others to follow.

Taylor's groundbreaking ideas began to take shape during his tenure at the Midvale Steel Company. Observing the inconsistent performance of workers, he identified that much of the inefficiency stemmed from a lack of clear direction and measurable objectives. To address this, Taylor developed time-motion studies, meticulously analyzing each step of a task to determine the most efficient way of completing it. By breaking down complex tasks into smaller, repeatable actions, he introduced the concept of "one best way" to perform work, eliminating guesswork and variability.

A key element of Taylor's scientific management was the emphasis on training and specialization. He believed that workers performed best when they were trained to execute a specific task with precision, rather than being expected to handle a broad range of duties. Taylor's approach required management to take an active role in designing workflows and ensuring workers adhered to standardized procedures. This shift not only improved consistency but also redefined the relationship between managers and employees, making the former responsible for guiding and optimizing labor rather than merely supervising it.

Despite its success in enhancing efficiency, Taylor's approach was not without controversy. Critics argued that his focus on productivity often came at the expense of workers' well-being. The emphasis on repetitive tasks, while effective in producing uniform results, led to monotony and a sense of alienation among workers. Taylor's methods were often seen as dehumanizing, reducing individuals to mere cogs in a machine. This tension highlighted the inherent trade-offs in his system: the pursuit of efficiency could sometimes undermine the human element of labor.

Nevertheless, Taylor's contributions laid the foundation for modern industrial management. His work influenced not only manufacturing but also sectors such as healthcare, education, and logistics, where standardized procedures became the norm. By advocating for a scientific approach to work, Taylor shifted the focus from subjective judgment to data-driven decision-making, setting the stage for innovations like Lean and Six Sigma. His legacy, while complex, underscores the transformative power of standardization in creating structured, scalable systems. Taylor's vision was not just about improving productivity—it was about demonstrating that work itself could be studied, understood, and perfected.

HENRY FORD: THE INNOVATOR OF THE ASSEMBLY LINE

Henry Ford revolutionized industrial production with his introduction of the assembly line, an innovation that transformed manufacturing and popularized the concept of mass production. While Frederick Taylor focused on optimizing individual tasks, Ford took these principles to a broader scale, creating a system that synchronized the efforts of workers and machines. This innovation not only increased efficiency but also made complex manufacturing accessible to a global audience, marking a turning point in industrial history.

Before Ford's assembly line, automobile production was a slow, labor-intensive process. Cars were hand-built by teams of skilled craftsmen, resulting in high costs and limited output. Ford recognized that to achieve his vision of making cars affordable for the average person, he needed to rethink the manufacturing process entirely. Inspired by concepts of division of labor and Taylor's scientific management, Ford developed a system where work would flow continuously, with each worker performing a specific task as the product moved down the line.

The first assembly line was introduced at Ford's Highland Park plant in 1913. It was a simple yet revolutionary concept: instead of workers moving to the product, the product came to the workers. By breaking down car assembly into smaller, standardized tasks, Ford drastically reduced production time. A Model T that once took over 12 hours to assemble could now be completed in less than 90 minutes. This dramatic improvement in efficiency not only allowed Ford to lower costs but also enabled mass production on an unprecedented scale, fundamentally altering the automobile industry.

Ford's assembly line was more than just a technical innovation; it was a social and economic game-changer. The efficiency gains allowed Ford to introduce the $5 workday in 1914, doubling the wages of his workers. This move, while controversial, was strategic. It reduced employee turnover, attracted a more skilled workforce, and gave workers greater purchasing power, effectively creating a new class of consumers. Ford's vision extended beyond production; he saw the assembly line as a means to democratize consumption, making products like the Model T accessible to millions and reshaping societal dynamics in the process.

However, the assembly line was not without its challenges. The repetitive nature of the work often led to worker dissatisfaction and burnout. Ford's emphasis on efficiency sometimes clashed with the human need for creativity and variety, leading to criticism that his system treated workers as interchangeable parts. Despite these limitations, the assembly line became a blueprint for industries worldwide, influencing sectors from electronics to agriculture. Ford's legacy lies not only in his technical innovation but also in his ability to see the broader implications of standardized processes, demonstrating how systematic approaches could redefine industries and societies alike.

LEGACY AND LESSONS LEARNED

The pioneering work of Frederick Taylor and Henry Ford laid the foundation for the industrialized world as we know it today. Their contributions revolutionized production processes, emphasizing efficiency, standardization, and scalability. Yet, their legacy extends far beyond the factory floor. By introducing methods that transformed how work was conceptualized, organized, and executed, they shaped modern business practices and set the stage for innovation in countless industries. Their achievements also provide critical lessons, both in their successes and the challenges they faced.

Taylor's scientific management brought structure to chaotic workplaces, demonstrating the value of methodical planning and data-driven decision-making. His emphasis on studying tasks and optimizing workflows introduced a new level of precision to work processes, a principle that continues to underpin modern management theories. Similarly, Ford's assembly line demonstrated the transformative power of process innovation, showing how efficiency at scale could make previously unattainable products accessible to the masses. Together, these contributions underscored the importance of viewing work as a system—one that can be analyzed, refined, and continually improved.

However, the legacy of Taylor and Ford is not without its controversies. Critics argue that their relentless pursuit of efficiency often overlooked the human dimension of labor. Taylor's focus on task optimization and Ford's regimented assembly lines, while effective, sometimes alienated workers, reducing their roles to monotonous, repetitive functions. This dehumanizing aspect highlighted a crucial limitation: systems that prioritize efficiency must also consider the well-being and engagement of the people who power them. The lessons here are clear—standardization must be balanced with flexibility and respect for the individual.

Another key takeaway from their work is the role of innovation in driving progress. Both Taylor and Ford were unafraid to challenge the status quo, introducing ideas that disrupted traditional ways of working. Their courage to experiment, adapt, and refine processes serves as a powerful reminder that transformative change often requires risk-taking and a willingness to reimagine established norms. For modern organizations, this lesson remains vital. Whether it's adopting new technologies, streamlining workflows, or rethinking organizational structures, continuous improvement is essential for staying competitive in an ever-changing landscape.

Their legacy underscores the importance of effective communication and leadership in implementing standardized processes. Taylor and Ford's systems succeeded because they were clearly defined, well-documented, and actively supported by management. They understood that for procedures to be embraced, they must be communicated in ways that engage and empower workers. This insight remains as relevant today as it was a century ago. Whether in factories, offices, or virtual teams, the ability to articulate a vision, align stakeholders, and foster collaboration is critical for translating standardization into sustained success.

In reflecting on the impact of Taylor and Ford, it becomes clear that their contributions were not just technical innovations but cultural milestones. They showed the world how structured approaches could transform industries, economies, and societies. While their methods evolved over time, the core principles they championed—efficiency, standardization, and continuous improvement—continue to shape the modern workplace. Their legacy is a testament to the enduring power of systematic thinking and a reminder that even the most groundbreaking ideas must be implemented with humanity and adaptability in mind.

The rise of international standards

The need for standardization arose as societies transitioned from localized production to industrialized economies in the late 19th and early 20th centuries. Before this shift, goods were often handcrafted or produced in small quantities, with no uniform specifications. This lack of standardization created inefficiencies, particularly as industries expanded and international trade began to flourish. The industrial revolution amplified this problem, introducing mass production and complex supply chains that required precise coordination. As global markets grew interconnected, the necessity for universal guidelines became increasingly apparent.

One of the earliest efforts to address this need came through national standardization bodies. The British Standards Institution (BSI), founded in 1901, was the first formal organization dedicated to creating consistent engineering and industrial standards. Its mission was clear: to ensure quality, safety, and compatibility in an era of rapid technological advancement. This concept quickly gained traction as other nations recognized the value of a unified approach to industrial practices. These early efforts laid the groundwork for international collaboration on standardization.

The global call for standardization culminated in the establishment of the International Federation of the National Standardizing Associations (ISA) in 1926, which aimed to coordinate technical standards across nations. Although ISA's efforts were interrupted by World War II, the need for international standards became even more urgent during the post-war reconstruction period. The rebuilding of war-torn economies and the rise of globalization highlighted the inefficiencies and risks of disparate systems. Countries realized that a unified standardization body could accelerate trade, reduce costs, and ensure interoperability.

In 1947, the International Organization for Standardization (ISO) was founded in Geneva, Switzerland, marking a pivotal moment in the history of standardization. Unlike its predecessor, the ISO was established with a broader mandate, encompassing all industries and technologies. Its mission was to create global standards that would harmonize practices across borders, facilitating seamless trade and collaboration. The name "ISO" was chosen not as an acronym but from the Greek word "isos," meaning equal, reflecting its goal of creating equal standards worldwide.

The introduction of ISO standards represented a paradigm shift. They enabled industries to transcend regional limitations, establishing universally accepted benchmarks for quality, safety, and performance. Standards like ISO 9001, introduced in 1987 for quality management, became critical tools for organizations seeking to compete on a global scale. Over time, these standards evolved to address emerging challenges, from environmental sustainability (ISO 14001) to information security (ISO 27001). This evolution not only reflected technological progress but also the growing interdependence of global economies.

Through the development of international standards, the world witnessed the power of collaboration in addressing complex challenges. Standardization emerged as a driving force for innovation, efficiency, and trust in global industries. The historical context of its birth underscores the necessity of unified approaches in navigating an increasingly interconnected world, a lesson that remains relevant today as organizations and nations face new challenges in an ever-changing global landscape.

ISO STANDARDS: A PILLAR OF GLOBALIZATION

The establishment of ISO standards revolutionized how industries operated, forming the backbone of globalization by creating a shared framework for quality, safety, and efficiency. Founded in 1947, the International Organization for Standardization (ISO) sought to unify industrial and commercial practices under universally accepted guidelines. The emergence of these standards was driven by the challenges of post-war reconstruction and the rapid expansion of international trade. For industries and governments alike, aligning to common standards became essential to navigate an increasingly interconnected world.

ISO standards brought a structured approach to addressing disparities in production methods and product specifications. Before their adoption, companies often struggled with inconsistent practices that hindered collaboration and market access. ISO's mission to harmonize these practices enabled businesses to streamline operations, reduce costs, and meet global expectations. Early standards focused on tangible aspects like product measurements and material properties, but their scope quickly expanded to encompass management systems and process optimization. This evolution demonstrated the adaptability of ISO standards to meet the changing needs of global industries.

A defining feature of ISO standards is their role in fostering trust in international commerce. For instance, ISO 9001, introduced in 1987, set a benchmark for quality management systems, requiring organizations to adopt consistent processes to ensure product and service quality. This standard became a hallmark of reliability, allowing businesses across diverse sectors—from manufacturing to healthcare—to demonstrate their commitment to excellence. Similarly, ISO 14001, focused on environmental management, established globally recognized principles for sustainability, helping companies align with growing environmental awareness and regulatory demands.

The impact of ISO standards extends beyond individual organizations, shaping entire industries and fostering cross-border collaboration. In sectors such as automotive, aerospace, and information technology, ISO standards have been instrumental in reducing inefficiencies and enhancing compatibility between global partners. For example, ISO/IEC 27001, addressing information security, has become vital for safeguarding digital assets in an era of increasing cyber threats. By providing a universally recognized framework, ISO standards enable seamless cooperation, reducing the barriers traditionally posed by differing regulatory environments and cultural practices.

Moreover, ISO's significance lies in its inclusive development process. Standards are created through consensus-building among experts from various fields, representing different countries and industries. This democratic approach ensures that the resulting guidelines are both practical and globally applicable. As a result, ISO standards not only reflect technical expertise but also embody the shared goals of diverse stakeholders. Their adoption continues to reinforce globalization by enabling organizations, regardless of size or geography, to compete and collaborate on a level playing field.

In a globalized economy, ISO standards have become synonymous with efficiency, reliability, and innovation. They provide a common language for industries to operate cohesively, empowering businesses to enter new markets with confidence. By addressing modern challenges such as environmental sustainability and cybersecurity, ISO remains a dynamic force in shaping the future of globalization, ensuring that progress is both inclusive and sustainable.

Lean Methodology: Streamlining Efficiency

Lean methodology, originating in the mid-20th century, transformed how organizations approached efficiency and value creation. Initially developed by Toyota in post-war Japan, Lean evolved from the company's efforts to maximize productivity while minimizing waste in a resource-constrained environment. Spearheaded by visionaries like Taiichi Ohno and Eiji Toyoda, this innovative system focused on optimizing workflows, reducing inefficiencies, and delivering maximum value to customers. Lean's principles, while deeply rooted in manufacturing, have since transcended industries, becoming a universal framework for operational excellence.

At the heart of Lean methodology lies the concept of eliminating waste, defined as any activity that does not add value to the final product or service. Waste, categorized into areas such as overproduction, waiting, and defects, was seen as a significant drain on resources and productivity. By systematically identifying and addressing these inefficiencies, Toyota pioneered a culture of continuous improvement, or *kaizen*, which empowered employees at every level to contribute to process optimization. This democratization of problem-solving was a cornerstone of Lean's success.

One of Lean's most influential contributions is the Just-In-Time (JIT) system, a production strategy aimed at delivering the right quantity of materials at the right time, thereby reducing inventory costs and ensuring a seamless workflow. JIT not only streamlined Toyota's operations but also set a new standard for efficiency in global manufacturing. Another hallmark of Lean is the principle of *jidoka*, or "automation with a human touch," which emphasizes stopping production to address quality issues immediately. These practices highlighted Lean's focus on quality and customer satisfaction as drivers of efficiency.

The influence of Lean methodology expanded beyond automotive manufacturing, finding applications in healthcare, software development, and supply chain management, among other fields. In healthcare, for instance, Lean principles have been used to reduce patient wait times, improve resource allocation, and enhance overall care quality. In software development, Lean has inspired practices like Agile, which prioritizes adaptability, customer collaboration, and iterative progress. These adaptations underscore Lean's versatility and relevance across diverse organizational contexts.

Lean methodology's enduring appeal lies in its holistic approach to efficiency. Rather than relying solely on technological advancements, Lean emphasizes cultural transformation and employee engagement. It encourages organizations to foster an environment of collaboration, transparency, and accountability, where every team member is invested in the continuous pursuit of excellence. By integrating Lean principles, businesses can not only enhance operational efficiency but also create a customer-centric ethos that drives long-term success.

In today's competitive landscape, Lean methodology remains a powerful tool for organizations striving to do more with less. Its principles of waste reduction, continuous improvement, and customer value provide a timeless framework for addressing modern challenges. By streamlining efficiency without compromising quality, Lean empowers organizations to innovate, adapt, and thrive in an ever-evolving global economy.

SIX SIGMA: DATA-DRIVEN EXCELLENCE

Six Sigma, introduced in the 1980s by Motorola, redefined how organizations approached quality control and operational efficiency. With its focus on data-driven decision-making, Six Sigma offered a structured methodology to reduce variability and defects in processes, ensuring consistent delivery of high-quality products and services. Built on the foundation of rigorous statistical analysis, Six Sigma represented a paradigm shift from traditional quality management practices to a comprehensive, analytical framework capable of addressing complex organizational challenges.

At its core, Six Sigma revolves around the concept of process improvement by identifying and eliminating causes of errors or inefficiencies. The term "Six Sigma" itself refers to achieving near-perfect process performance, allowing only 3.4 defects per million opportunities. This ambitious standard necessitated the adoption of advanced statistical tools and methodologies to scrutinize every aspect of production or service delivery. By doing so, Six Sigma provided a roadmap for achieving operational excellence and elevating customer satisfaction to unprecedented levels.

The DMAIC framework—Define, Measure, Analyze, Improve, and Control—is the backbone of Six Sigma's methodology. This structured approach guides organizations through the process of problem identification, root cause analysis, and sustainable solution implementation. For example, in manufacturing, the Measure and Analyze phases involve collecting extensive data on production processes to uncover bottlenecks or inconsistencies, while the Improve phase focuses on implementing targeted interventions to address these issues. The Control phase ensures that improvements are maintained over time, embedding a culture of quality within the organization.

One of Six Sigma's distinguishing features is its reliance on trained specialists, known as Green Belts, Black Belts, and Master Black Belts, who lead projects and drive process improvements. These roles highlight Six Sigma's commitment to building internal expertise, equipping organizations with the skills needed to sustain continuous improvement. This investment in human capital has made Six Sigma a transformative force, fostering innovation and accountability at every organizational level.

The impact of Six Sigma has extended across industries, from manufacturing to healthcare, finance, and beyond. In healthcare, Six Sigma has been used to reduce medical errors, improve patient outcomes, and optimize resource allocation. In finance, it has helped organizations streamline processes like loan approvals and risk management, leading to cost savings and enhanced customer experiences. Its adaptability and results-oriented approach have made Six Sigma a preferred methodology for organizations seeking to balance efficiency with quality.

Ultimately, Six Sigma's emphasis on data, precision, and continuous improvement has made it a cornerstone of modern business excellence. By integrating statistical rigor with practical solutions, Six Sigma empowers organizations to overcome challenges, seize opportunities, and deliver consistent value to stakeholders. In a world where quality and efficiency are non-negotiable, Six Sigma's principles remain as relevant and impactful as ever, driving innovation and excellence across industries.

THE GLOBAL IMPACT OF STANDARDIZATION

Standardization has fundamentally reshaped the global economy, bridging gaps between industries, cultures, and regions while fostering innovation and efficiency. The adoption of universal standards has enabled seamless collaboration across borders, allowing companies to align processes, ensure compatibility, and drive progress on a global scale. By establishing a shared framework for quality, safety, and sustainability, standardization has become an essential pillar of international commerce and development, uniting diverse stakeholders under common objectives.

One of the most significant impacts of standardization is its ability to facilitate trade and market access. Before the widespread implementation of standards, industries faced challenges due to inconsistent practices, regulations, and expectations. With frameworks such as ISO standards, Lean methodology, and Six Sigma, businesses can now operate under unified guidelines, reducing barriers to entry and fostering trust among global partners. Standardization has been particularly transformative in industries like manufacturing and technology, where consistent specifications are critical for interoperability and performance.

Standardization has also played a crucial role in advancing innovation by providing a foundation for collaboration and shared knowledge. For instance, the telecommunications industry relies on standardized protocols to ensure devices and networks from different manufacturers can work together seamlessly. Similarly, in sectors like pharmaceuticals and medical devices, adherence to global standards ensures that products meet rigorous safety and efficacy requirements, enabling lifesaving innovations to reach markets worldwide. This harmonization has accelerated the pace of technological advancement while ensuring accountability and consumer protection.

The environmental and social dimensions of standardization are equally significant. With growing awareness of climate change and sustainability, standards such as ISO 14001 and ISO 26000 have provided organizations with practical tools to address environmental and social challenges. These frameworks encourage companies to adopt sustainable practices, reduce waste, and engage in ethical operations, aligning business goals with global priorities. By promoting responsible practices, standardization contributes to broader efforts to achieve sustainable development and address pressing global issues.

Despite its many benefits, standardization also faces challenges, particularly in ensuring inclusivity and adaptability. As global economies evolve, standards must remain dynamic to address emerging needs and incorporate diverse perspectives. Critics argue that over-standardization can stifle creativity or disproportionately benefit established players, highlighting the need for a balanced approach. Nevertheless, the ongoing refinement of standards through collaborative efforts ensures their relevance and continued impact, reflecting the collective aspirations of industries and societies worldwide.

In the 21st century, the global impact of standardization is evident in its ability to create opportunities, drive efficiency, and promote a shared vision of progress. By fostering trust, enabling collaboration, and addressing global challenges, standardization has become a cornerstone of modern industry and society. Its influence transcends sectors and borders, uniting diverse actors in pursuit of a more interconnected, sustainable, and innovative world.

Lessons from early successes and failures in standardization

The early successes in standardization laid the groundwork for the sophisticated systems we rely on today. By creating consistency in processes, materials, and outputs, pioneers demonstrated how standardization could drive efficiency, reduce costs, and enable scalability. These achievements were not merely technical advancements but pivotal shifts in how industries approached production and operations, ultimately reshaping global commerce and innovation.

One of the most notable early successes was the development of interchangeable parts in manufacturing during the late 18th and early 19th centuries. Eli Whitney's application of this principle in producing muskets for the U.S. military revolutionized the arms industry. By ensuring that each component was uniform and could fit into any assembly of the same product, Whitney dramatically reduced production time and costs. This breakthrough marked the beginning of mass production, showcasing the power of standardization to achieve unprecedented levels of efficiency.

The railroad industry also exemplified the transformative potential of early standardization efforts. During the 19th century, disparate rail gauges— the width between rails—created significant inefficiencies and barriers to seamless travel and trade. The eventual adoption of standardized gauges in many regions facilitated the integration of rail networks, boosting commerce and enabling industrial growth. This success was not only a technological milestone but also a testament to the economic and logistical benefits of unifying standards across competing entities.

Henry Ford's introduction of the assembly line further cemented the value of standardization. By breaking down complex tasks into smaller, repeatable steps and using standardized components, Ford made automobile production faster and more cost-effective than ever before. The Model T, a symbol of this innovation, became an affordable vehicle for the masses, transforming transportation and consumer culture. Ford's approach demonstrated that standardization could democratize access to goods and services while driving industrial efficiency to new heights.

These early triumphs revealed key elements essential to successful standardization: clear objectives, technological innovation, and alignment with broader economic and social goals. They also underscored the importance of collaboration, as many of these successes required collective buy-in from stakeholders across industries. By establishing a shared vision and fostering cooperation, early standardization efforts not only achieved immediate goals but also set the stage for ongoing advancements.

Through these foundational successes, industries learned that standardization was more than a tool for efficiency—it was a strategic framework for growth, innovation, and collaboration. These principles remain as relevant today as they were during the industrial revolution, reminding us that well-executed standards can unlock transformative potential in any field.

FAILURES IN STANDARDIZATION: MISSTEPS AND OVERSIGHTS

While the promise of standardization has often driven innovation and efficiency, its history also includes notable failures that underscore the complexity of implementing universal practices. Missteps in execution, resistance to change, and overreliance on rigid frameworks have, at times, led to inefficiencies, conflicts, and stagnation. These failures offer valuable lessons, revealing the critical need for balance, foresight, and adaptability in the pursuit of standardization.

One prominent example of failure lies in the early attempts to standardize telecommunication systems across Europe in the mid-20th century. As various countries pursued their own national standards for phone networks, cross-border communication became cumbersome and inefficient. The lack of coordination delayed the development of integrated systems, creating significant challenges for businesses operating across borders. This fragmented approach to standardization ultimately necessitated extensive retrofitting and renegotiation, wasting time and resources that could have been avoided with a more collaborative initial strategy.

Another misstep can be seen in the automotive industry's initial efforts to standardize emission controls. In the 1960s and 1970s, divergent regulatory frameworks in the United States, Europe, and Asia led to conflicting standards for vehicle manufacturers. Automakers were forced to develop region-specific designs, increasing costs and limiting scalability. The failure to establish a unified global standard for emissions not only hindered industry efficiency but also delayed meaningful environmental progress. This situation highlighted how competing interests and a lack of global consensus can undermine the benefits of standardization.

Rigid adherence to standards has also been a source of failure in some cases. In the construction industry, for example, strict compliance with outdated building codes has, at times, stifled innovation and hindered the adoption of sustainable materials and practices. This overemphasis on uniformity, without room for context or evolution, reveals the danger of treating standards as static rather than dynamic tools. When standardization fails to adapt to new challenges or technologies, it risks becoming a barrier rather than a facilitator of progress.

Cultural and organizational resistance to change has further compounded standardization failures. In industries where workers perceive standardization as a top-down imposition rather than a collaborative improvement, initiatives have often faced pushback. For example, early attempts to standardize workflows in healthcare met with resistance from practitioners who viewed them as bureaucratic constraints rather than enhancements to patient care. This resistance underscores the importance of stakeholder engagement and clear communication in driving successful standardization efforts.

These missteps and oversights reveal that standardization is not a one-size-fits-all solution. Its success depends on thoughtful implementation, continuous refinement, and a deep understanding of the context in which it is applied. Failure to anticipate resistance, account for diverse needs, or remain adaptable can turn even the most well-intentioned initiatives into costly lessons. However, by learning from these failures, organizations can develop more inclusive, flexible, and effective approaches to standardization, ensuring it serves as a catalyst for growth and innovation rather than a source of friction.

THE ROLE OF CONTEXT IN SUCCESS AND FAILURE

The effectiveness of standardization depends heavily on the context in which it is applied. While the principles of creating uniformity and efficiency are universal, the specific needs, challenges, and cultural environments of industries, regions, and organizations can shape outcomes significantly. The ability to adapt standards to these unique conditions often determines whether they become tools for progress or sources of friction.

One of the most illustrative examples of context-driven success is Toyota's adaptation of Lean Manufacturing principles. Rooted in the cultural ethos of Japan, Lean emphasized waste reduction, continuous improvement, and respect for employees at all levels. These practices resonated deeply within Toyota's organizational culture, which valued teamwork and long-term thinking. However, when other companies outside Japan sought to replicate Toyota's success, they often struggled to achieve similar results. Without aligning Lean methodologies with their own cultural and operational realities, many organizations implemented them superficially, missing the underlying values that made them effective.

Conversely, some failures in standardization highlight the dangers of ignoring contextual factors. The introduction of universal healthcare documentation standards in the United States serves as a case in point. While these standards aimed to streamline record-keeping and improve patient care, their initial implementation failed to consider the diverse technological capabilities and workflows of healthcare providers. Smaller clinics, in particular, found the requirements burdensome, as they lacked the resources to adapt quickly. The result was widespread frustration, inefficiencies, and delayed adoption, ultimately undermining the initiative's objectives.

Global trade offers another lens through which the role of context becomes evident. The International Organization for Standardization (ISO) has been instrumental in creating technical and quality benchmarks that facilitate cross-border commerce. However, the application of ISO standards in developing countries has sometimes been met with resistance. Local businesses, often constrained by limited resources, struggle to meet these standards, perceiving them as barriers rather than enablers. Without initiatives to provide support and capacity-building, the broader benefits of such standards can remain inaccessible, leading to economic disparities rather than integration.

Context is not only shaped by geography or industry but also by timing and technological advancement. In the early days of standardizing internet protocols, efforts like the adoption of TCP/IP succeeded largely because they emerged during a period of collaborative enthusiasm among engineers and researchers. Had these protocols been proposed in a more commercially competitive or fragmented environment, their acceptance might have been delayed or derailed. This example underscores the importance of aligning standardization efforts with the prevailing social, economic, and technological conditions.

The role of context in standardization underscores the need for flexibility and inclusivity. Successful initiatives require careful assessment of the environments in which they are implemented, as well as ongoing dialogue with stakeholders to ensure alignment with their needs. When context is ignored, even the most well-conceived standards risk alienating those they aim to serve. However, when standards are designed with adaptability and collaboration at their base, they have the potential to bridge gaps, foster innovation, and drive lasting progress across diverse settings.

Core Lessons for Contemporary Standardization

The evolution of standardization offers a wealth of lessons for its contemporary application, underscoring the balance between consistency and adaptability. As industries grow more interconnected and technology advances at an unprecedented pace, the challenge lies in creating frameworks that remain relevant while fostering innovation. Contemporary efforts can draw valuable insights from past successes and failures to navigate this complex terrain effectively.

One crucial lesson is the importance of stakeholder inclusion. Successful standardization initiatives recognize that collaboration between all affected parties—governments, organizations, employees, and consumers—ensures broader acceptance and practicality. The development of modern safety standards for autonomous vehicles exemplifies this principle. By engaging car manufacturers, regulators, and technology firms, these standards aim to address both safety concerns and technological feasibility. This inclusive approach prevents top-down mandates that might overlook key operational or cultural considerations, aligning standards with real-world needs.

Flexibility is another main principle that contemporary standardization must embrace. While uniformity is essential, rigid adherence to outdated standards can stifle growth and fail to accommodate new developments. For instance, the rapid rise of e-commerce has necessitated continual updates to payment security standards like PCI DSS to address emerging cybersecurity threats. Organizations that adapt these frameworks in response to evolving challenges not only remain compliant but also build consumer trust. Flexibility ensures that standards remain dynamic tools rather than static roadblocks.

Global alignment is increasingly vital in today's interconnected world. The standardization of mobile communication protocols, such as the rollout of 5G, highlights the power of global consensus. By aligning technical requirements across countries, this initiative has accelerated deployment, reduced costs, and created a seamless user experience. However, this success is tempered by geopolitical tensions, which sometimes hinder the creation of universal frameworks. The lesson here is that fostering international cooperation requires both diplomacy and shared economic incentives to overcome barriers.

Another critical takeaway is the role of education and communication in standardization. For standards to be effective, those implementing and affected by them must understand their purpose and benefits. The adoption of ISO 14001 environmental standards in businesses has been most successful when accompanied by training programs that emphasize their value in sustainability and cost reduction. Clear communication ensures that standards are not perceived as bureaucratic hurdles but as tools for improvement, fostering buy-in at all levels of an organization.

A forward-thinking mindset is essential. Effective standardization anticipates future needs rather than merely addressing current challenges. For example, standards for renewable energy integration into power grids are being developed to support the long-term transition to sustainable energy sources. By considering emerging trends and potential disruptions, standardization efforts can remain relevant and proactive.

Core lessons for contemporary standardization revolve around adaptability, inclusivity, and foresight. Whether applied in technology, manufacturing, healthcare, or any other sector, these principles ensure that standards evolve alongside the needs of a rapidly changing world. By learning from historical experiences and embracing the complexities of modern contexts, contemporary standardization can drive innovation, enhance collaboration, and address global challenges with precision and purpose.

BUILDING ON THE PAST: A BLUEPRINT FOR THE FUTURE

The history of standardization provides a rich foundation for envisioning its future, offering both cautionary tales and aspirational successes. As industries and societies confront new challenges—ranging from climate change to technological disruption—the need for well-conceived, adaptable standards has never been more urgent. A blueprint for future standardization begins with a commitment to learning from the past while addressing the demands of an interconnected, rapidly evolving world.

One of the key lessons from historical successes is the importance of aligning standardization efforts with universal values and goals. For example, the early adoption of safety standards in manufacturing was driven by a shared desire to protect workers and improve productivity. Today, global standards must similarly reflect collective priorities such as sustainability, equity, and technological innovation. Efforts like the United Nations' Sustainable Development Goals (SDGs) demonstrate how international collaboration can create frameworks that address diverse yet interconnected challenges, such as environmental conservation and social justice. By grounding new standards in widely accepted principles, their relevance and adoption can be significantly enhanced.

Another pillar for the future of standardization is the integration of advanced technologies. Unlike the industrial pioneers of the past, contemporary efforts have access to tools like artificial intelligence, blockchain, and the Internet of Things (IoT). These technologies can streamline the creation, implementation, and monitoring of standards. For instance, blockchain can ensure transparency and accountability in supply chains, reinforcing adherence to ethical and quality standards. Similarly, AI-powered analytics can identify inefficiencies and areas for improvement, enabling standards to evolve dynamically based on real-time data. Embracing these tools will ensure that standardization remains agile and capable of addressing complex, multidimensional challenges.

Inclusivity is another critical component of this blueprint. In the past, standardization often excluded marginalized groups or smaller organizations, inadvertently widening socioeconomic divides. Future efforts must prioritize accessibility and equity, ensuring that all stakeholders—regardless of size, region, or resources—have a voice in the process. Initiatives like the Fairtrade certification system highlight how inclusive standardization can create economic opportunities for small producers while addressing global issues such as ethical sourcing and sustainability. By fostering collaboration across diverse sectors and demographics, future standards can achieve broader impact and legitimacy.

A forward-looking blueprint must also emphasize education and capacity building. Standards cannot succeed if they are not understood or embraced by those expected to implement them. Investing in training programs, accessible resources, and clear communication will ensure that standards are not just theoretical constructs but practical tools for improvement. For example, programs designed to help small and medium-sized enterprises (SMEs) meet international standards have proven effective in increasing global trade participation. Similarly, equipping workers with the knowledge to apply and adapt standards fosters innovation and engagement, turning compliance into a shared endeavor rather than an imposed obligation.

The future of standardization must embrace continuous improvement. Just as the pioneers of standardization refined their methods over time, modern efforts must remain iterative and responsive. Regular reviews, stakeholder feedback, and the ability to sunset outdated standards are essential for maintaining relevance and effectiveness. Organizations like ISO already incorporate such practices, updating their guidelines to reflect new insights and technological advancements. Building a culture of ongoing refinement ensures that standards evolve in step with the changing needs of industries, societies, and the planet.

By building on the successes and failures of the past, future standardization efforts can chart a path that is inclusive, innovative, and impactful. With a focus on universal values, technological integration, and continuous learning, standardization can serve as a powerful catalyst for progress, bridging divides and fostering global collaboration in an increasingly complex world. This blueprint is not merely a roadmap but a call to action, urging industries, governments, and individuals to engage in shaping the standards that will define the future.

The hidden benefits of well-defined processes

In every workplace, whether in a bustling corporate office or a small freelance operation, the processes we follow often determine the success we achieve. These procedures, though sometimes seen as mundane or overly bureaucratic, serve as the invisible scaffolding that supports efficiency, quality, and growth. Without them, even the most innovative ideas can falter, caught in the chaos of inconsistent execution or avoidable errors. Yet, despite their significance, many people fail to recognize the true value of well-defined processes until they encounter a breakdown that disrupts their goals.

Consider the frustration of a team facing unclear roles during a project deadline. Tasks overlap, deadlines slip, and finger-pointing ensues—all because there was no process in place to define responsibilities and ensure smooth coordination. This isn't an isolated scenario; such inefficiencies plague organizations of all sizes and industries. What's often misunderstood is that effective processes aren't restrictive—they're liberating. They free teams to focus on creativity and strategic decision-making by eliminating the friction of ambiguity and disorganization.

Work procedures are much more than a set of instructions or checklists. At their foundation, they embody an organization's collective knowledge, refined through experience and aimed at optimizing performance. They are the bridge between lofty strategic ambitions and the practical steps needed to achieve them. Without this bridge, even the best ideas can remain unrealized, lost in the gap between planning and execution.

The benefits of well-defined procedures extend beyond individual efficiency or team productivity. When implemented thoughtfully, they create a foundation for sustained success, ensuring not only smoother operations but also better outcomes and scalable growth. Whether it's ensuring compliance in regulated industries, maintaining quality in complex production processes, or simply saving time in everyday tasks, well-structured procedures prove indispensable.

This section delves into the hidden advantages of clearly defined work processes. By examining how they enhance efficiency, ensure consistent quality, and enable growth, we'll uncover why they are not merely tools for order but essential drivers of innovation and achievement. Understanding these benefits is the first step in transforming procedures from perceived constraints into powerful assets for personal and organizational success.

KEY BENEFIT 1: EFFICIENCY

Efficiency lies at the heart of every thriving organization. It is the ability to achieve maximum results with minimum wasted effort, time, or resources. While innovation and creativity often capture the spotlight, it is efficiency—the quiet enabler—that keeps businesses running smoothly and consistently. Well-defined processes serve as the backbone of this efficiency, ensuring that every action contributes meaningfully to the organization's objectives without unnecessary detours or delays.

Fundamentally, a well-defined process eliminates ambiguity. In workplaces without clear procedures, employees often spend valuable time figuring out what needs to be done, how to do it, or who is responsible for specific tasks. This lack of clarity leads to duplicated efforts, missed deadlines, and, ultimately, frustration. In contrast, processes that clearly outline roles, steps, and expectations enable individuals and teams to proceed with confidence and precision. For example, in a customer service department, a structured escalation process ensures that issues are routed to the right personnel swiftly, reducing response times and enhancing customer satisfaction.

Efficiency is not just about speed; it's also about consistency. Clear processes help reduce the learning curve for new employees and ensure that tasks are completed uniformly, regardless of who is handling them. This uniformity minimizes errors and allows organizations to produce reliable outcomes, even in high-pressure situations. In manufacturing, for instance, standardized procedures can mean the difference between a seamless production line and one riddled with costly errors. A single misstep in a poorly defined process might lead to defects, delays, or wasted materials.

Moreover, efficient processes free up time and resources for innovation. When employees are not bogged down by inefficiencies, they have more bandwidth to think strategically, solve problems creatively, and pursue new opportunities. For instance, companies that automate routine tasks, such as payroll processing or inventory tracking, often find that their teams can focus on higher-value activities like customer engagement or product development. The efficiency derived from clear processes thus has a multiplier effect, benefiting both operational performance and strategic growth.

Lastly, efficiency creates a culture of trust and reliability. When employees know that processes are well-designed and consistently applied, they are more likely to trust the system and each other. This trust reduces workplace stress and fosters collaboration, as individuals can focus on their contributions without constantly worrying about procedural gaps or missteps. In this way, efficiency, powered by well-defined processes, becomes more than a productivity tool—it becomes a foundation for a cohesive and empowered workforce.

KEY BENEFIT 2: QUALITY

Quality is a cornerstone of success in any field, from manufacturing and service delivery to creative industries and freelance work. High-quality output builds trust with clients, customers, and stakeholders, fostering loyalty and long-term relationships. Achieving consistent quality, however, is not a matter of chance—it requires deliberate effort, systems, and oversight. Well-defined processes are instrumental in ensuring this consistency, acting as a safeguard against errors and a roadmap for achieving excellence.

When processes are clearly defined, they provide a standard for performance that all team members can follow. This standardization reduces variability in outcomes, ensuring that each product, service, or deliverable meets the expected level of quality. For example, a restaurant chain with detailed preparation procedures ensures that diners enjoy the same meal quality regardless of location. Similarly, an e-commerce company with streamlined packaging protocols minimizes shipping errors, preserving customer satisfaction. By removing guesswork, these processes turn quality into a reliable and repeatable achievement.

Another critical way well-defined processes enhance quality is by embedding checks and balances into workflows. Quality control measures, such as regular audits, peer reviews, or automated testing, can be seamlessly integrated into structured processes. In the software development industry, for instance, using predefined coding standards and automated testing protocols allows teams to identify bugs early and maintain high-quality code. These built-in safeguards help detect issues before they escalate, reducing rework and ensuring that deliverables meet or exceed expectations.

Processes also facilitate continuous improvement, a key driver of sustained quality. By tracking adherence to procedures and analyzing outcomes, organizations can identify inefficiencies or shortcomings and refine their methods over time. This iterative approach is evident in industries like healthcare, where well-documented processes allow for the collection of data that can improve patient outcomes. For instance, hospitals with standardized treatment protocols can monitor recovery rates, adjust practices based on findings, and achieve higher levels of care.

Well-defined processes foster accountability, which is integral to maintaining quality. When roles and responsibilities are clearly outlined, individuals understand their contributions to the larger goal and are more likely to take ownership of their tasks. This sense of accountability reduces oversight lapses and encourages meticulous attention to detail. In creative agencies, for example, having a structured review process for content ensures that all work is polished and aligned with client expectations before it is delivered.

In essence, quality is not a one-time achievement but an ongoing commitment. Well-defined processes provide the structure and support needed to uphold this commitment, ensuring that organizations can consistently deliver value to their stakeholders. Whether through standardization, safeguards, iterative improvement, or accountability, these processes transform the pursuit of quality from an aspiration into a sustainable reality.

Key Benefit 3: Scalability

Scalability is the ability of an organization or system to grow and adapt effectively without compromising performance or quality. For businesses aspiring to expand their reach, serve more customers, or increase their operational capacity, scalability is a critical goal. However, growth often amplifies inefficiencies and exposes weaknesses in existing workflows. This is where well-defined processes become indispensable, acting as the foundation for sustainable and controlled expansion.

A clear and standardized process ensures that workflows remain efficient and manageable as the scope of operations increases. Without a structured approach, scaling can lead to chaos—roles become unclear, tasks are overlooked, and communication breaks down. Consider a startup transitioning from a team of five to a staff of fifty. Without processes to guide onboarding, project management, and task delegation, the organization risks losing the agility that initially made it successful. Well-defined procedures enable teams to replicate successful practices across new hires or departments, preserving efficiency and consistency even as the organization grows.

Scalable processes also allow for easier integration of new technologies and systems. As businesses expand, they often turn to automation and digital tools to manage increased workloads. For these tools to be effective, underlying workflows must be well-documented and standardized. For instance, an online retailer implementing an automated inventory system relies on predefined processes for categorizing, tracking, and restocking products. Without this structure, automation efforts might falter, creating more confusion than they solve.

Moreover, well-defined processes provide a roadmap for training and development, which are vital for scaling a workforce. As organizations grow, they must onboard new employees quickly and effectively, ensuring they can contribute productively from the start. A company with clear training manuals, step-by-step guides, and documented workflows can reduce the learning curve for new hires. This is particularly crucial for franchises or multinational organizations where uniformity in service delivery is a key competitive advantage.

Processes also serve as a stabilizing force during periods of rapid change. Scaling often introduces new challenges, from increased customer demands to the complexities of managing a larger team. Clear procedures mitigate these growing pains by providing a reliable framework that employees can follow even in uncertain times. For example, a consulting firm expanding to multiple regions can maintain its reputation for quality service by adhering to standardized project management protocols across all offices.

Ultimately, scalability hinges on the ability to balance growth with stability. Well-defined processes make this possible by enabling organizations to replicate their successes, integrate new systems seamlessly, and maintain quality as they scale. Whether it's a small business aspiring to enter new markets or a global corporation managing exponential growth, these processes transform the ambition to grow into a strategic reality. They ensure that expansion doesn't come at the cost of efficiency, quality, or organizational coherence, making them an essential tool for sustainable success.

Work procedures are often underestimated, dismissed as rigid or overly bureaucratic, yet their impact on organizational success is profound. As we have seen, well-defined processes are not merely tools for maintaining order—they are enablers of efficiency, quality, and scalability, the core drivers of sustainable growth. By eliminating ambiguity and streamlining workflows, these processes allow teams to focus on creativity and problem-solving. They provide the structure necessary for achieving consistent, high-quality results and form the foundation for growth that is both scalable and resilient.

Through the lens of efficiency, processes emerge as time-savers and productivity enhancers, cutting through the chaos of disorganization and wasted effort. They enable individuals and teams to work smarter, not harder, creating a smoother flow of operations that leads to better outcomes. When it comes to quality, procedures act as guardians of consistency, embedding standards and checkpoints into workflows to minimize errors and maximize reliability. Scalability, the third pillar, reveals the transformative power of processes in preparing organizations to expand without losing their edge. Together, these benefits highlight why structured workflows are not a limitation but a catalyst for success.

Understanding the importance of these key benefits is only the beginning. For processes to truly deliver on their potential, they must be designed with intention, implemented thoughtfully, and adapted over time. Organizations that treat processes as living systems—open to feedback and refinement—unlock their ability to evolve alongside changing needs. This adaptability ensures that procedures remain relevant and effective, no matter how complex or dynamic the environment becomes.

The transition from viewing processes as constraints to recognizing them as strategic tools requires a mindset shift. It calls for leaders, teams, and even individuals to embrace the idea that structure and creativity are not mutually exclusive. When aligned with organizational goals, well-defined processes amplify innovation, empower people, and foster collaboration. They turn the abstract into the actionable, helping bridge the gap between vision and execution.

In the sections to come, we will delve deeper into how to create, refine, and implement effective work procedures tailored to your unique needs. From identifying inefficiencies to fostering buy-in and collaboration, the following chapters will equip you with the tools to turn procedures into a competitive advantage. By embracing the principles of clarity, adaptability, and continuous improvement, you can transform work processes into a cornerstone of your personal and organizational success.

How procedures ensure compliance and mitigate risk in regulated industries

In regulated industries, compliance is not just a requirement—it is a critical pillar of operations that determines an organization's ability to function, compete, and sustain its reputation. Industries such as healthcare, finance, aviation, and pharmaceuticals are governed by strict laws and guidelines designed to protect public safety, ensure ethical conduct, and foster consumer trust. These regulations are not arbitrary; they often stem from lessons learned through significant failures, ranging from financial scandals to public health crises. Compliance, therefore, is more than a legal checkbox—it is a commitment to integrity and accountability that safeguards both the organization and the wider community.

Failure to comply with industry regulations can have severe consequences, extending far beyond fines or legal action. Non-compliance often damages an organization's reputation, leading to loss of trust from customers, investors, and stakeholders. For example, major financial institutions involved in money laundering scandals face billions in penalties, but the real cost lies in the erosion of public confidence. Similarly, pharmaceutical companies that bypass regulatory standards may face lawsuits and product recalls, with lasting impacts on their credibility. These examples illustrate that compliance is intrinsically tied to an organization's survival and success.

The complexities of compliance grow exponentially as industries globalize and regulatory frameworks evolve. Organizations operating across borders must navigate a patchwork of regulations, each with its own nuances and requirements. For instance, a multinational company in the food industry must adhere to food safety standards in every country where it operates. This means understanding and implementing processes that comply with the FDA in the United States, EFSA regulations in Europe, and equivalent bodies elsewhere. The stakes are further heightened by the possibility of regulatory updates, which require businesses to remain agile and vigilant.

At the heart of maintaining compliance in these high-stakes environments are robust procedures. These are the tools that translate legal requirements into day-to-day practices, ensuring that employees understand and adhere to the necessary standards. Procedures provide clarity, eliminating ambiguity about what needs to be done and how it should be executed. For example, in the aviation industry, standardized checklists for pre-flight inspections ensure that safety protocols are followed meticulously. By embedding compliance into routine workflows, procedures reduce the risk of human error and create a culture of responsibility.

Ultimately, compliance in regulated industries is a shared responsibility that extends from leadership to frontline employees. While senior executives establish policies and ensure alignment with legal requirements, it is through well-defined procedures that these policies take effect. Without this structural foundation, even the most diligent organizations can falter. Compliance is not simply about avoiding penalties; it is a proactive measure to build resilience, protect stakeholders, and uphold the values that define the organization. As the foundation of this effort, procedures are indispensable, linking regulatory demands to actionable, enforceable practices.

THE ROLE OF PROCEDURES IN ENSURING COMPLIANCE

Procedures play a pivotal role in ensuring compliance by transforming complex regulatory requirements into clear, actionable steps that can be consistently followed across an organization. Regulatory frameworks are often dense and intricate, making it difficult for individuals to interpret and apply them effectively. Without structured guidance, even the most well-intentioned employees may inadvertently deviate from the rules, putting the organization at risk. Procedures bridge this gap, serving as a practical tool for translating abstract regulations into tangible practices that align with legal and industry standards.

One of the key ways procedures ensure compliance is by fostering uniformity and consistency across operations. In industries like pharmaceuticals or manufacturing, consistency is critical not only for meeting regulatory requirements but also for maintaining quality and safety. For instance, Good Manufacturing Practices (GMP) in the pharmaceutical sector mandate strict adherence to processes for production, storage, and distribution. Detailed procedures outlining each step ensure that products are manufactured consistently and meet regulatory standards, minimizing the risk of contamination or defects. This uniformity is particularly vital in industries where even minor deviations can have severe consequences.

Documentation is another essential component of compliance, and procedures are integral to ensuring accurate and thorough record-keeping. Regulatory bodies often require organizations to demonstrate their adherence to standards through audits, inspections, or certifications. Without properly documented procedures, organizations may struggle to provide the necessary evidence, leading to penalties or a loss of operating licenses. For example, in the financial sector, anti-money laundering (AML) regulations require institutions to maintain detailed records of customer transactions. Procedures that mandate systematic documentation enable these organizations to remain audit-ready while also building a robust compliance framework.

Procedures also play a preventive role in compliance by embedding safeguards that mitigate the risk of violations. In healthcare, for instance, adherence to protocols for patient data privacy under regulations like HIPAA (Health Insurance Portability and Accountability Act) protects both patients and providers. These protocols outline specific measures, such as encrypting sensitive information and limiting access to authorized personnel, thereby reducing the likelihood of data breaches. Similarly, safety protocols in industries like oil and gas include procedures for handling hazardous materials and responding to emergencies, ensuring compliance with environmental and workplace safety regulations.

Procedures create a culture of accountability and awareness within organizations, encouraging employees to internalize the importance of compliance. By providing clear instructions and expectations, procedures empower employees to act responsibly and confidently within the bounds of regulatory frameworks. Training programs often rely on these procedures to educate staff, reinforcing their understanding of compliance obligations. Over time, this procedural foundation fosters a proactive approach to compliance, where employees not only follow the rules but also identify and address potential risks before they escalate.

Procedures are the backbone of compliance, translating the complexity of regulations into manageable, actionable practices. They provide the structure necessary to maintain consistency, ensure accountability, and reduce risk, allowing organizations to navigate the ever-evolving regulatory landscape with confidence and integrity.

PROCEDURES AS TOOLS FOR RISK MITIGATION

Risk is an inherent part of any organization's operations, but in regulated industries, its consequences can be particularly severe. Whether the risk involves financial losses, legal penalties, or harm to public safety, failing to manage it effectively can undermine an organization's stability and reputation. Procedures are one of the most effective tools for risk mitigation, offering a structured approach to identifying, assessing, and addressing potential threats. By embedding risk management directly into daily workflows, well-defined procedures create a proactive shield against vulnerabilities, safeguarding both the organization and its stakeholders.

At their center, procedures enable organizations to anticipate risks by standardizing how potential issues are identified and assessed. This systematic approach ensures that risks are not left to chance or subjective interpretation. For example, in the construction industry, safety protocols often include regular site inspections and hazard assessments. These procedures establish a clear process for identifying risks such as unstable scaffolding or exposed electrical wiring, allowing teams to address these dangers before they lead to accidents. By institutionalizing risk identification, procedures reduce reliance on individual vigilance and create a more reliable defense against unforeseen events.

Mitigating risk also requires swift and appropriate responses when threats are detected, and this is another area where procedures are invaluable. They provide predefined actions for managing incidents, ensuring consistency and clarity in high-pressure situations. Take, for instance, the aviation industry, where emergency response procedures are critical to passenger safety. Pilots and crew follow detailed protocols for handling scenarios such as engine failure or cabin depressurization. These procedures not only guide their actions but also instill confidence in their ability to manage crises effectively, minimizing the impact of potentially catastrophic events.

Beyond addressing immediate threats, procedures play a preventative role by embedding safeguards into routine operations. In industries like finance, this often involves implementing checks and balances to detect irregularities. For example, anti-fraud procedures might require dual authorization for large transactions, reducing the likelihood of financial misconduct. Similarly, in manufacturing, quality assurance processes include rigorous testing and inspection steps that prevent defective products from reaching consumers. By introducing such preventative measures, procedures reduce exposure to risks that could escalate into costly or damaging outcomes.

Procedures also help organizations adapt to changing risk landscapes by incorporating feedback loops and continuous improvement mechanisms. As industries evolve, so too do the risks they face, whether due to technological advancements, market shifts, or regulatory changes. Well-designed procedures are not static; they are updated regularly to reflect new challenges and lessons learned from past incidents. For example, cybersecurity procedures in the tech industry often evolve in response to emerging threats, such as ransomware or phishing attacks. By remaining dynamic and adaptable, these procedures ensure that organizations are always prepared for the risks of tomorrow.

Procedures act as a safety net, providing both structure and flexibility in managing risks. They create a culture of vigilance and accountability, where employees understand their roles in preventing and responding to potential threats. By turning risk management into an integrated, organization-wide effort, procedures not only minimize vulnerabilities but also build resilience, enabling organizations to weather challenges and emerge stronger. Far from being mere operational tools, they are strategic assets that protect the foundation of any business operating in a complex and uncertain world.

CHALLENGES IN MAINTAINING COMPLIANCE THROUGH PROCEDURES

While procedures are vital for ensuring compliance, maintaining their effectiveness in dynamic environments presents significant challenges. Regulatory landscapes are constantly evolving, with new laws, standards, and guidelines emerging in response to societal, technological, and environmental shifts. Organizations must adapt their procedures accordingly, but the pace and complexity of change can make this a daunting task. Without regular updates and strategic foresight, even the most robust procedures risk becoming obsolete, leaving organizations exposed to non-compliance.

One of the primary challenges lies in balancing standardization with flexibility. Procedures are designed to provide consistency, yet rigid adherence can hinder an organization's ability to adapt to unique situations or unexpected challenges. For instance, a pharmaceutical company may have detailed protocols for clinical trials, but unforeseen circumstances—such as a sudden pandemic—might demand adjustments that fall outside existing frameworks. Organizations that fail to build adaptability into their procedures may find themselves caught between regulatory requirements and operational realities, struggling to maintain compliance without compromising efficiency.

Another hurdle is the human element inherent in the application of procedures. Employees at all levels are responsible for implementing these processes, yet gaps in training, communication, or awareness can lead to errors or non-compliance. For example, a financial institution may have strict procedures for identifying and reporting suspicious transactions under anti-money laundering (AML) regulations. However, if staff lack adequate training or fail to understand the importance of these steps, critical risks may go unnoticed. Ensuring that procedures are effectively communicated, understood, and followed requires ongoing investment in education and engagement.

The global nature of many industries further complicates compliance efforts. Organizations operating across multiple jurisdictions must navigate varying regulatory frameworks, often with conflicting requirements. Consider the food industry, where companies must adhere to differing safety standards in the European Union, United States, and Asia. Standardizing procedures to meet these diverse regulations is not only resource-intensive but also fraught with the risk of misinterpretation or oversight. Moreover, cultural differences in how rules are perceived and followed can exacerbate these challenges, requiring tailored approaches to procedural implementation and enforcement.

Technology, while a powerful enabler of compliance, also introduces its own set of challenges. Digital tools such as automated workflows, compliance management systems, and artificial intelligence can streamline procedures and reduce human error. However, reliance on technology is not without risks. Software malfunctions, cyberattacks, or data breaches can compromise compliance efforts, particularly in industries handling sensitive information such as healthcare or finance. Organizations must ensure that their technological solutions are secure, regularly updated, and integrated seamlessly with their procedural frameworks to avoid introducing new vulnerabilities.

Maintaining compliance through procedures requires organizational buy-in and a culture that values adherence to regulations. Resistance to change, whether from leadership or frontline employees, can undermine the effectiveness of even the most well-designed processes. This resistance often stems from a perception that procedures are bureaucratic burdens rather than tools for operational excellence. Overcoming this mindset requires transparent communication about the purpose and benefits of compliance, as well as visible support from leadership to champion procedural adherence.

Despite these challenges, organizations that proactively address these barriers can transform procedural compliance into a competitive advantage. By investing in adaptability, employee education, global awareness, technological robustness, and cultural alignment, they can maintain not only compliance but also resilience in an increasingly complex regulatory environment. This approach underscores the importance of viewing procedures as dynamic, evolving assets rather than static rules, ensuring their relevance and effectiveness over time.

THE BUSINESS CASE FOR COMPLIANCE AND RISK-ORIENTED PROCEDURES

Compliance and risk-oriented procedures are not just regulatory necessities; they are strategic investments that safeguard an organization's reputation, financial stability, and operational continuity. Beyond avoiding fines or penalties, these procedures can enhance trust with stakeholders, foster operational efficiency, and provide a competitive edge in the marketplace. For organizations in regulated industries, the business case for robust compliance and risk management processes lies in their ability to transform potential vulnerabilities into sources of strength and resilience.

One of the most immediate benefits of compliance-oriented procedures is their role in protecting an organization from costly penalties and legal action. Regulatory violations often result in significant financial consequences, ranging from fines to suspended operations. For instance, non-compliance with environmental regulations in industries like manufacturing or energy production can lead to multi-million-dollar penalties, tarnishing both profitability and public image. Adhering to well-defined procedures ensures that organizations remain within legal boundaries, avoiding such disruptions and preserving resources for growth and innovation.

Reputation management is another critical component of the business case for compliance. In an age where corporate accountability is under constant scrutiny, public perception can make or break an organization. Scandals or compliance failures can erode trust among customers, investors, and partners, leading to long-term damage that far outweighs the immediate financial costs. Conversely, organizations that demonstrate a commitment to compliance—by adhering to ethical labor practices, protecting consumer data, or reducing environmental impact—enhance their credibility and appeal. These benefits translate into stronger brand loyalty, increased investor confidence, and a competitive advantage in securing partnerships or contracts.

Risk-oriented procedures also support operational efficiency by preventing disruptions and streamlining decision-making. A clear framework for managing risks reduces uncertainty and enables faster, more informed responses to emerging challenges. For example, in the supply chain sector, procedures designed to address risks such as supplier delays or geopolitical instability help ensure continuity of operations. By proactively addressing potential bottlenecks, organizations minimize downtime and maintain steady production, ultimately reducing costs and enhancing customer satisfaction. This alignment of compliance with operational goals underscores the value of integrating risk management into everyday workflows.

The strategic alignment fostered by compliance and risk management procedures further enhances an organization's ability to innovate and grow.

While compliance is often perceived as a constraint, it can also act as a catalyst for improvement. Adhering to stringent standards in regulated industries frequently drives technological advancements, process optimization, and the development of safer, higher-quality products. For instance, the aerospace industry's rigorous safety protocols have spurred innovations in materials, engineering, and testing methodologies, elevating both industry standards and competitive positioning. By leveraging compliance as a driver for excellence, organizations can turn regulatory challenges into opportunities for differentiation.

Finally, compliance and risk-oriented procedures contribute to long-term resilience, enabling organizations to withstand disruptions and adapt to changing conditions. In a world marked by rapid technological evolution, shifting regulatory landscapes, and increasing societal expectations, the ability to manage risks effectively is paramount. Procedures that prioritize compliance ensure that organizations are not only prepared for current challenges but also equipped to navigate future uncertainties. This proactive approach fosters sustainable growth, allowing businesses to thrive in competitive and volatile markets.

The business case for compliance is clear: organizations that prioritize robust, risk-oriented procedures position themselves for sustained success. Far from being a burden, these processes create a foundation for trust, efficiency, innovation, and resilience, ensuring that organizations can achieve their strategic goals while meeting their regulatory obligations. By embracing compliance as a strategic imperative rather than a checkbox exercise, businesses can unlock value and build a legacy of reliability and excellence.

Compliance and risk-oriented procedures are often seen as restrictive mandates imposed by external forces, yet their true value lies in the stability and strategic advantage they provide. In today's interconnected and highly regulated global environment, these procedures are not merely operational necessities; they are enablers of trust, efficiency, and long-term success. By addressing both compliance and risk management, organizations create a solid framework that protects their operations, fosters innovation, and enhances their reputation.

As explored, the role of procedures extends far beyond mitigating fines or avoiding legal repercussions. They ensure operational continuity, promote ethical practices, and strengthen relationships with stakeholders, including customers, employees, and regulators. By embedding compliance and risk management into their core processes, organizations can shift from a reactive posture to a proactive approach, viewing regulations and risks as opportunities for growth rather than obstacles to overcome. This transformation is not just beneficial—it is essential in a competitive and ever-changing marketplace.

A critical takeaway is that compliance and risk-oriented procedures are not static. To remain effective, they must evolve with the regulatory landscape, technological advancements, and organizational priorities. This adaptability requires an ongoing commitment to review, revise, and refine processes to address emerging risks and meet new standards. Organizations that embrace this mindset position themselves as agile and forward-thinking leaders in their industries, capable of thriving amidst uncertainty.

Transitioning from understanding the importance of compliance and risk management to implementing practical strategies is the next logical step. Organizations must consider how to align their procedures with both regulatory demands and business objectives. This includes fostering a culture of accountability and transparency, investing in training and technological tools, and establishing mechanisms for continuous feedback and improvement. By doing so, businesses can ensure that their procedures remain not only relevant but also impactful.

The discussion now shifts to actionable strategies for integrating compliance and risk management into everyday workflows. By examining the practical methods for building, implementing, and refining procedures, organizations can bridge the gap between theory and execution. These strategies will empower readers to take control of their compliance efforts, transforming procedures from bureaucratic necessities into powerful instruments for operational excellence and organizational resilience.

Bridging the gap between strategic goals and daily execution.

In the modern workplace, a common challenge emerges when grand organizational strategies fail to translate into actionable outcomes. Leaders invest significant effort into crafting visions that promise innovation, growth, or transformation. Yet, as these ambitions cascade down through layers of management and teams, the clarity of intent often dissipates, leading to fragmented execution and diluted results. This phenomenon, known as the vision-execution disconnect, is not a failure of ideas but rather of the mechanisms needed to bridge the gap between strategy and action.

The disconnect is particularly evident in organizations operating across multiple departments, regions, or disciplines. For example, a company may set a strategic goal of increasing market share by 20% within a year. While the leadership team may envision bold marketing campaigns or customer-centric product innovations, operational teams may struggle to translate these objectives into their daily workflows. Sales staff might focus on hitting their existing quotas, production teams might prioritize cost efficiency, and marketing may lack a clear directive for aligning their efforts. The result is a lack of cohesion that undermines the overarching goal.

This gap is not merely theoretical—it has tangible consequences. Misaligned execution can lead to wasted resources, missed opportunities, and employee frustration. Teams may feel disconnected from the larger purpose of their work, leading to a decline in morale and productivity. Furthermore, stakeholders, from investors to customers, may perceive inconsistency or inefficiency, eroding trust and confidence in the organization's ability to deliver on its promises. The stakes are high, and addressing this issue requires more than motivational speeches or revised mission statements.

The root of the vision-execution disconnect often lies in the absence of clear and consistent procedures. Without defined processes, the journey from strategy to execution becomes riddled with ambiguity. Employees at various levels are left to interpret high-level goals without a structured framework, resulting in varied and often conflicting approaches. This lack of standardization creates bottlenecks and inefficiencies, ultimately stalling progress and diminishing outcomes.

This chapter explores how organizations can overcome the vision-execution disconnect by leveraging well-designed procedures. By translating strategic goals into specific, measurable, and actionable steps, these processes serve as the bridge that connects leadership's vision to the daily efforts of teams and individuals. They ensure alignment, consistency, and momentum, enabling organizations to not only dream big but also execute effectively. This foundational understanding sets the stage for examining the transformative role of procedures in achieving strategic success.

THE STRATEGIC ROLE OF PROCEDURES

Procedures play a pivotal role in translating high-level strategic goals into tangible actions, ensuring that every layer of an organization contributes cohesively to its overarching objectives. At their core, procedures serve as the operational blueprint that connects a vision—often abstract and aspirational—with the day-to-day activities that drive progress. Without these structured frameworks, even the most well-crafted strategies risk remaining aspirational ideals, disconnected from measurable outcomes.

The strategic function of procedures begins with their ability to distill complex goals into actionable steps. For instance, an organization aiming to enhance customer satisfaction might outline a strategy emphasizing faster response times and improved service quality. This broad objective, while clear in intention, can mean different things to different teams. Procedures eliminate ambiguity by defining specific actions, such as setting maximum response time targets, implementing customer feedback loops, and providing staff with training schedules. This granular breakdown ensures that everyone understands their role in achieving the goal, creating alignment across the organization.

Moreover, procedures promote accountability by clarifying expectations at every level. When strategic goals are embedded into daily tasks through well-defined processes, employees have a clear understanding of their responsibilities and how their efforts contribute to broader objectives. For example, a sales team following a structured process for lead management can track how their activities influence revenue growth, ensuring alignment with corporate financial targets. This visibility fosters a sense of ownership, motivating individuals and teams to deliver results that support organizational goals.

Procedures also act as the foundation for scalability, a critical component of strategic growth. When organizations expand into new markets, launch additional product lines, or increase operational capacity, their ability to maintain consistency and efficiency hinges on well-established processes. Standardized procedures ensure that strategic goals can be replicated and adapted across different contexts, preserving quality and coherence even as the organization evolves. For example, a retail chain's procedural guidelines for inventory management enable seamless integration of new locations without compromising the customer experience.

Procedures facilitate the alignment of diverse teams, functions, and geographies, uniting them under a shared purpose. In large, complex organizations, the lack of alignment often leads to silos, where teams pursue their own objectives without regard for the bigger picture. Procedures bridge these gaps by establishing common practices, terminologies, and metrics that everyone adheres to. For instance, in a multinational corporation, standardized reporting procedures ensure that data collected across regions can be compared and analyzed to inform global strategies.

The strategic role of procedures is both foundational and transformative. By translating vision into action, fostering accountability, enabling scalability, and ensuring alignment, they empower organizations to move cohesively toward their goals. Procedures are not merely tools for maintaining order—they are instruments of strategic execution that connect ambition with achievement, creating a roadmap for success that is as precise as it is practical.

ENHANCING TEAM ALIGNMENT THROUGH PROCESSES

Team alignment is one of the most critical factors in achieving organizational success, yet it is often undermined by fragmented communication, conflicting priorities, and siloed operations. Procedures offer a structured approach to overcoming these barriers by creating a common language and shared understanding across diverse teams. By establishing clarity, promoting collaboration, and ensuring consistency, processes become the foundation for aligning efforts toward shared objectives.

One of the key ways processes enhance alignment is by eliminating ambiguity. In the absence of clear procedures, teams often interpret goals and responsibilities differently, leading to miscommunication and inefficiencies. For example, consider a product launch involving marketing, sales, and development teams. Without a standardized process detailing deliverables, timelines, and handoff points, each group may focus on their interpretation of priorities, resulting in delays or missed targets. Defined procedures provide a roadmap, ensuring that all teams understand their roles, the interdependencies between their tasks, and the ultimate objectives.

Processes also foster collaboration by creating structured opportunities for interaction and feedback. In cross-functional projects, differing perspectives can either be a source of innovation or a point of contention, depending on how they are managed. Procedures that outline regular meetings, feedback loops, and escalation pathways encourage open communication while minimizing conflict. For instance, a company implementing an agile project management process ensures that all stakeholders contribute to sprint planning and retrospective reviews, creating a culture of collaboration where team members feel heard and valued.

Furthermore, processes build trust among teams by establishing transparency and fairness. When procedures are clear and consistently applied, they reduce perceptions of favoritism or bias. For example, a performance review process that includes standardized metrics and defined timelines ensures that every team member is evaluated against the same criteria. This transparency fosters trust in leadership and strengthens relationships among colleagues, as everyone feels they are operating on a level playing field.

Alignment is also reinforced through shared metrics and reporting procedures. When teams operate with consistent key performance indicators (KPIs) and standardized reporting formats, it becomes easier to monitor progress and identify areas for improvement. For example, in a sales and marketing alignment initiative, a common process for tracking leads from generation to conversion ensures that both teams work toward the same revenue targets. This shared focus on measurable outcomes not only aligns efforts but also highlights the impact of collaboration, motivating teams to work together more effectively.

Processes support adaptability, ensuring that alignment is maintained even in the face of change. Organizations often encounter shifting priorities, whether due to market dynamics, technological advancements, or leadership decisions. Well-designed processes incorporate mechanisms for revisiting and revising plans, allowing teams to realign quickly without losing momentum. For instance, a technology company employing iterative development processes can pivot to address emerging customer needs while ensuring that all teams remain on the same page.

Enhancing team alignment through processes is not just about improving communication or clarifying roles—it is about creating a cohesive, high-performing organization where every effort is directed toward a common purpose. By fostering clarity, collaboration, trust, shared accountability, and adaptability, procedures bridge the gaps that often divide teams, transforming potential discord into coordinated action. This alignment lays the groundwork for seamless execution, driving organizations closer to their strategic goals with every step.

BRIDGING METRICS AND DAILY ACTIVITIES

Metrics serve as the compass for organizational success, providing measurable indicators of progress toward strategic goals. However, their true value is realized only when they are meaningfully connected to the daily activities of teams and individuals. Bridging the gap between high-level metrics and day-to-day tasks requires deliberate effort and well-defined processes, ensuring that every action contributes directly to organizational outcomes.

At the crux of this connection is the principle of translation: converting abstract performance indicators into tangible, actionable steps. For instance, if a company's key metric is improving customer satisfaction scores by 15% within a year, frontline employees must understand how their actions influence this target. Processes such as standardized customer service protocols or response time guidelines provide clear directives on what team members can do daily to impact this metric. By breaking down broad goals into smaller, actionable elements, processes make success accessible and measurable at every level.

Procedures also create alignment by establishing accountability frameworks tied to metrics. When tasks and responsibilities are clearly defined within a process, it becomes easier to track how individual and team efforts contribute to organizational goals. For example, a sales department aiming to increase quarterly revenue may adopt a process that sets weekly targets for outreach and follow-ups. Regularly reviewing these activities against revenue metrics provides a feedback loop, enabling employees to see the direct correlation between their daily efforts and the organization's financial performance.

In addition, processes ensure consistency in how metrics are pursued across teams and geographies. Large organizations often struggle with discrepancies in how goals are interpreted and implemented, leading to uneven performance. Standardized procedures, such as shared workflows and reporting formats, eliminate these variations. For instance, a global logistics company might use a uniform process for tracking on-time delivery rates across all regions. This consistency not only supports accurate measurement but also ensures that every team is working toward the same standards of performance.

Technology plays a crucial role in bridging metrics and activities, and its integration into processes amplifies their effectiveness. Tools such as dashboards, project management software, and data analytics platforms make metrics visible and actionable for employees. A marketing team, for example, might use a dashboard displaying real-time campaign performance metrics. By embedding these tools into daily workflows, processes ensure that employees can monitor their contributions to key performance indicators (KPIs) and adjust their activities as needed.

Processes foster a culture of continuous improvement by linking metrics to iterative reviews and refinements. When daily activities are evaluated against metrics in regular intervals, organizations gain valuable insights into what is working and what needs adjustment. For example, a manufacturing plant might employ a process where production metrics are reviewed weekly to identify inefficiencies. Over time, these reviews lead to optimized workflows, driving incremental improvements that cumulatively enhance overall performance.

The bridge between metrics and daily activities is not merely a conduit for information; it is a dynamic framework that transforms strategy into execution. By translating metrics into actionable tasks, fostering accountability, ensuring consistency, leveraging technology, and promoting continuous improvement, processes ensure that organizational goals are not only understood but actively pursued at every level. This connection empowers teams to see the direct impact of their efforts, fostering a sense of purpose and driving sustained success.

ADAPTING PROCEDURES TO EVOLVING STRATEGIES

Organizations operate in an environment of constant change, driven by shifting market demands, technological advancements, and evolving customer expectations. As strategies adapt to these dynamics, so must the procedures that underpin their execution. Static or outdated processes can hinder growth, create inefficiencies, and disconnect teams from strategic goals. The ability to align procedures with evolving strategies is a hallmark of resilient and forward-thinking organizations.

The first step in adapting procedures is recognizing when change is needed. This requires continuous monitoring of external trends and internal performance metrics to identify misalignments between strategy and execution. For example, a retail company expanding its online presence might notice that its traditional inventory management processes are ill-suited to e-commerce operations. By reviewing these procedures in light of new strategic priorities, the organization can proactively make adjustments before inefficiencies escalate.

Flexibility is essential in updating procedures to match strategic shifts. Organizations often fall into the trap of overstandardizing processes, making them rigid and resistant to change. While consistency is important, adaptability must also be built into procedural design. For instance, a company adopting a hybrid work model may need to revise its procedures for team collaboration. Allowing room for iterative feedback during the rollout of new collaboration tools ensures that the process evolves based on real-world challenges and successes.

The integration of technology is a critical enabler of procedural adaptability. Digital tools allow organizations to quickly update, disseminate, and implement new processes, ensuring alignment with strategic goals. For example, a software development firm transitioning to an agile methodology might use cloud-based project management platforms to redefine workflows in real time. These tools not only simplify the adaptation process but also provide data insights that inform further refinements, creating a feedback loop between strategy and execution.

Employee engagement is another cornerstone of adapting procedures effectively. Changes in strategy often ripple through an organization, requiring buy-in from teams at every level. When employees are involved in the process of revising procedures, they are more likely to embrace and implement them successfully. For example, a financial services company revamping its compliance procedures might host workshops where employees contribute insights based on their frontline experiences. This collaborative approach ensures that new procedures are both practical and aligned with strategic objectives.

Organizations must institutionalize periodic reviews of procedures to ensure they remain relevant as strategies evolve. These reviews should be scheduled as part of broader strategic planning cycles, creating a natural rhythm for assessing and updating processes. For instance, a healthcare organization might align its procedural reviews with annual evaluations of patient care standards, ensuring that its operational practices keep pace with advancements in medical technology and treatment protocols.

Adapting procedures to evolving strategies is not a one-time effort but an ongoing commitment to agility and alignment. By recognizing the need for change, designing flexible processes, leveraging technology, engaging employees, and institutionalizing periodic reviews, organizations can ensure that their procedures remain a powerful enabler of strategic success. In a world where change is the only constant, this adaptability transforms procedural frameworks into dynamic assets that drive sustained performance and growth.

FROM STRATEGY TO EXECUTION: TURNING VISION INTO REALITY

Bridging the gap between strategic goals and daily execution is a challenge faced by organizations of all sizes and industries. The journey from vision to reality is fraught with obstacles, yet it is also where success is forged. At the heart of this transformation lies the ability to align processes with goals, ensuring that every task contributes meaningfully to the broader mission.

As explored throughout this discussion, the disconnect between strategy and execution often stems from unclear priorities, inconsistent communication, and a lack of actionable frameworks. Procedures, when thoughtfully designed and implemented, provide the structure and guidance necessary to overcome these barriers. They transform high-level objectives into specific, repeatable actions, creating a cohesive pathway from intention to impact.

A key takeaway is the transformative power of well-aligned processes. They not only improve operational efficiency and team alignment but also ensure that metrics and activities are directly linked to organizational goals. These connections foster clarity, accountability, and motivation, empowering employees to see their role in achieving the company's vision. Through adaptable and feedback-driven frameworks, procedures also enable organizations to stay agile in the face of evolving strategies and external disruptions.

However, the success of any procedural framework depends on its ability to resonate with those who implement it. Teams need to feel engaged and valued in the process of procedural design and adaptation. This human element is what turns processes from abstract rules into actionable tools that inspire commitment and creativity. By fostering collaboration and emphasizing the shared purpose behind procedures, organizations can build a culture that views processes not as constraints, but as enablers of success.

As we transition to the practical application of these ideas, the next step is to explore how organizations can systematically develop, refine, and adapt procedures to ensure their enduring relevance and impact. This involves diving deeper into the tools, strategies, and case studies that illustrate procedural excellence in action. From setting up feedback loops to leveraging technology and fostering continuous improvement, these practices will bridge the theoretical insights of this discussion with actionable guidance that readers can apply in their unique contexts.

In the end, turning vision into reality requires more than ambition—it demands a commitment to aligning strategy with execution through thoughtful, adaptable processes. With the right framework in place, organizations can navigate complexity, drive results, and bring their strategic aspirations to life. Let's explore how to make this a practical reality in the chapters to come.

Making Procedures Work for You

In any organization, the effectiveness of work procedures profoundly impacts its capacity to meet goals, adapt to change, and foster innovation. Yet, these procedures often operate unnoticed in the background until something goes wrong—deadlines are missed, resources are wasted, or employees become frustrated. Identifying gaps and inefficiencies in these procedures is not merely a reactionary measure; it is a proactive approach to ensuring that an organization remains resilient and competitive in an ever-changing landscape. The value lies not just in addressing immediate issues but in uncovering opportunities for improvement that might otherwise remain hidden.

At its core, identifying procedural gaps is about seeing the organization as a living system, where every process connects to others in a complex web. When a single part of that system is inefficient, the effects ripple outward, often in unexpected ways. For instance, a delay in procurement might not only hold up production but also strain relationships with clients awaiting delivery. These inefficiencies, while seemingly small in isolation, can snowball into significant challenges. Recognizing and addressing them before they escalate is a hallmark of thoughtful management and a critical step in building long-term sustainability.

The importance of identifying gaps also extends to the human element of work. Employees often bear the brunt of flawed procedures, facing bottlenecks, unclear expectations, or redundant tasks that hinder productivity. Over time, this can lead to disengagement, frustration, and even burnout. Conversely, a workplace that prioritizes identifying and addressing inefficiencies fosters a culture of continuous improvement. When employees see that their challenges are being acknowledged and addressed, they are more likely to feel valued and empowered, contributing to a more engaged and motivated workforce.

From a strategic perspective, the ability to pinpoint inefficiencies is directly tied to an organization's capacity for innovation. Gaps in procedures often reveal outdated methods or blind spots that have persisted simply because "that's how it's always been done." By interrogating these gaps, organizations can find pathways to innovation—whether through adopting new technologies, rethinking workflows, or streamlining operations. Identifying gaps is not just about fixing what is broken; it is about reimagining what could be possible.

The process of identifying inefficiencies serves as a foundation for resilience in a rapidly evolving world. Economic shifts, technological advancements, and changing consumer expectations demand agility, and agility begins with knowing where the organization stands. A clear understanding of current procedures and their limitations provides the insight needed to adapt quickly and effectively to new challenges. By recognizing the importance of identifying gaps, organizations position themselves not only to survive disruptions but to thrive in their aftermath.

COMMON SIGNS OF PROCEDURAL INEFFICIENCIES

Procedural inefficiencies often manifest in ways that are easy to overlook but profoundly impact organizational performance when left unaddressed. One of the most apparent signs is delays—whether in project timelines, service delivery, or decision-making processes. These delays often point to bottlenecks in workflows, where tasks are dependent on one person, department, or step that consistently falls behind. For example, if approvals require multiple layers of sign-off without clear accountability or streamlined processes, they can slow down progress and frustrate those waiting for decisions. Identifying such delays requires more than observing missed deadlines; it involves understanding the root causes embedded in procedural structure.

Another significant indicator is redundancy, where work is unnecessarily duplicated or repeated due to a lack of clarity or communication. Redundancies often occur in teams where roles and responsibilities are not well-defined, leading to overlap in efforts. For instance, two departments may unknowingly undertake similar tasks because there is no unified system for sharing information. Similarly, employees might be required to enter the same data into multiple systems due to incompatible tools or poorly integrated technologies. Such inefficiencies not only waste time and resources but also reduce morale by creating a sense of futility among team members.

Recurring errors or quality issues are also red flags signaling procedural inefficiencies. When mistakes happen consistently, it often means that the underlying process is flawed rather than the individuals executing it. These errors might result from unclear instructions, inadequate training, or tools that do not meet the needs of the task. For example, an invoicing system prone to manual input errors could indicate a need for automation or better checks. Addressing these inefficiencies requires analyzing not only the errors themselves but also the conditions that enable them, ensuring the focus shifts from blaming individuals to improving systems.

Employee frustration and disengagement frequently stem from procedural inefficiencies, serving as a more subjective but equally telling sign. When employees find themselves hindered by unnecessary steps, ambiguous processes, or lack of resources, their productivity and satisfaction can suffer. Complaints about "too much red tape" or requests for "more efficient tools" are often indicators of deeper procedural issues. Over time, this frustration can erode trust in leadership, as employees may perceive inefficiencies as a sign of mismanagement or disregard for their needs. Listening to these concerns is critical to uncovering inefficiencies that might not be immediately visible in metrics.

Lastly, inefficiencies can be detected through discrepancies in outcomes versus expectations. When performance metrics consistently fall short despite adequate resources and effort, it often points to misaligned or poorly designed processes. For example, a sales team might fail to meet targets because of a cumbersome client-onboarding procedure that delays lead conversion. Such gaps highlight the need for a closer examination of workflows to ensure they align with the desired goals. By paying attention to these signs—whether quantitative, like delays and errors, or qualitative, like employee frustration—organizations can begin to uncover the procedural inefficiencies that hinder their success.

STEPS TO ANALYZE EXISTING PROCEDURES

Analyzing existing procedures is a vital process for any organization seeking to enhance its efficiency, minimize errors, and create value through optimized workflows. The first step in this analysis is creating a clear and comprehensive map of the current processes. This involves documenting every step within the procedure, identifying the individuals or teams involved, and understanding the sequence of tasks. Tools like flowcharts or process maps are invaluable here, as they provide a visual representation of workflows that can highlight redundancies, bottlenecks, or unnecessary steps. Without a clear understanding of how the procedure functions in its entirety, any attempt at improvement risks addressing symptoms rather than root causes.

Once the process is mapped, the next step is to gather input from stakeholders who interact with the procedure regularly. This includes frontline employees, managers, and even external partners, depending on the scope of the process. Each group offers unique insights into what works, what doesn't, and where inefficiencies may lie. Employees often know where the procedure causes delays or confusion but might not feel empowered to voice their concerns without a formal review process. Encouraging open and honest feedback is crucial, as it reveals nuances that might be missed by external observers or higher-level managers.

After collecting feedback, the analysis should turn to measuring the outcomes of the existing procedures against predefined benchmarks or goals. This involves examining metrics such as time taken to complete tasks, error rates, or customer satisfaction scores. If these metrics consistently fall below expectations, it suggests that the procedure is not functioning optimally. For instance, if a process intended to resolve customer complaints within 48 hours routinely takes longer, this points to an issue requiring immediate attention. Analyzing outcomes not only helps identify where the procedure is falling short but also sets a baseline for measuring the success of future improvements.

A critical element in this process is identifying the root causes of inefficiencies. Using methodologies such as Root Cause Analysis (RCA) or the "Five Whys" technique, organizations can delve deeper into the underlying issues rather than just addressing surface-level symptoms. For example, if a manufacturing line frequently experiences delays, RCA might reveal that the problem is not with worker productivity but with inconsistent supply deliveries. Understanding these root causes ensures that solutions are targeted and effective, reducing the likelihood of recurring problems.

The analysis should conclude with a structured evaluation of potential tools and technologies that could address the identified gaps. In today's rapidly evolving technological landscape, solutions such as workflow automation, task management software, or advanced analytics tools can transform inefficient procedures into streamlined operations. However, it's essential to ensure that any tools introduced align with the organization's needs and capabilities. A poorly chosen technology can exacerbate inefficiencies rather than resolve them. By carefully analyzing existing procedures through these structured steps, organizations can uncover actionable insights that form the foundation for meaningful, sustainable improvements.

Framework for Identifying Gaps

A structured framework for identifying gaps in work procedures is essential to systematically uncover inefficiencies and build a foundation for meaningful improvements. This framework begins with defining the scope and objectives of the analysis, ensuring a focused approach tailored to the specific needs of the organization or team. The scope should clarify which processes will be analyzed, their boundaries, and the desired outcomes of the review. For example, an organization seeking to improve customer onboarding might limit the analysis to the initial 30-day interaction cycle, with an objective of reducing delays and enhancing user satisfaction. Without a defined scope, the analysis risks becoming too broad or misaligned with strategic priorities.

The next step in the framework is process mapping, which provides a detailed visualization of the current workflows. This involves charting out each step, decision point, and handoff in the procedure, as well as identifying the actors—both human and technological—involved. Process mapping can be conducted using tools such as SIPOC diagrams (Supplier, Input, Process, Output, Customer) or swimlane diagrams that show the roles of various stakeholders. This exercise often highlights areas where tasks are duplicated, unnecessary steps exist, or decision points slow down the workflow. By breaking the process into its constituent elements, organizations gain a clear view of where gaps may lie.

Stakeholder engagement is a critical element of the framework. Procedures often appear efficient from a managerial or theoretical standpoint but fail in execution due to practical challenges experienced by those who implement them. Employees, team leads, and even customers who interact with the process bring invaluable perspectives to the analysis. Conducting interviews, focus groups, or anonymous surveys allows stakeholders to share their experiences, frustrations, and suggestions for improvement. These insights not only reveal inefficiencies but also foster a sense of inclusion, encouraging buy-in for future procedural changes.

Another pillar of the framework is data-driven analysis. Quantitative metrics such as cycle time, error rates, resource utilization, and cost efficiency provide a measurable foundation for identifying gaps. For instance, tracking how long it takes to complete a specific step in the process can uncover bottlenecks, while analyzing error frequencies may point to unclear instructions or inadequate training. In addition, qualitative data, such as customer complaints or employee feedback, enriches the analysis by providing context to the numbers. A combination of these data sources ensures a holistic understanding of where and why gaps exist.

The framework incorporates root cause identification, a step that ensures the analysis does not stop at surface-level symptoms. Techniques like Ishikawa diagrams (fishbone diagrams) or Pareto analysis can help pinpoint the fundamental issues underlying procedural inefficiencies. For example, a bottleneck in production might initially appear to stem from a lack of manpower, but further analysis could reveal outdated equipment as the true cause. Root cause identification allows organizations to develop targeted, effective solutions rather than applying temporary fixes. By following this structured framework, organizations can systematically identify gaps, ensuring a thorough and actionable foundation for improving their work procedures.

To illustrate how identifying and addressing procedural gaps can transform an organization, consider the example of a mid-sized e-commerce company struggling with customer order fulfillment. Despite having a growing customer base and an efficient-looking workflow on paper, the company was receiving frequent complaints about delayed shipments and incorrect orders. These issues were not only eroding customer trust but also increasing operational costs due to returns and expedited shipping to correct errors. Recognizing the urgency, the company embarked on a thorough review of its fulfillment process to pinpoint the root causes of these inefficiencies.

The first step involved mapping the entire order fulfillment process, from when a customer placed an order to when the package was delivered. This exercise revealed several bottlenecks, including delays in the handoff between the inventory team and the packaging department. Orders were frequently stuck in the queue because inventory checks were conducted manually and lacked real-time updates, leading to confusion about product availability. Furthermore, packaging labels were printed in batches instead of on demand, causing delays during peak times when large numbers of orders needed processing simultaneously.

Next, the company gathered feedback from employees across departments involved in the fulfillment process. The warehouse staff reported that they often wasted time searching for items because the inventory system did not accurately reflect their physical locations. Packaging team members highlighted frequent errors in order details, which required double-checking and rework. Customer service representatives shared that many complaints stemmed from miscommunication about delivery timelines, exacerbated by an outdated tracking system that provided inaccurate updates. These insights from various stakeholders painted a clearer picture of the systemic issues at play.

Armed with this information, the company analyzed performance metrics to validate the feedback. Data showed that orders were delayed by an average of two days due to the inventory bottleneck, and nearly 15% of orders contained errors linked to mismatched product details. Further investigation revealed that these inefficiencies were costing the company a significant portion of its profit margin. Using root cause analysis tools like Pareto charts, the team prioritized addressing the inventory and labeling issues, as they accounted for the majority of delays and errors.

To resolve these gaps, the company implemented a series of targeted improvements. A barcode-based inventory management system was introduced, allowing real-time tracking of stock levels and item locations. This eliminated the confusion and delays caused by manual checks. Additionally, the company adopted a print-on-demand system for packaging labels, ensuring faster processing during high-volume periods. Training sessions were conducted for employees to familiarize them with the new tools and processes, and regular feedback loops were established to monitor the effectiveness of the changes.

Within six months, the results were remarkable. Order delays dropped by 50%, error rates fell to under 5%, and customer satisfaction scores improved significantly. The changes not only resolved immediate problems but also laid the groundwork for scalability as the company continued to grow. This example demonstrates how a systematic approach to identifying procedural gaps—combining mapping, stakeholder input, data analysis, and targeted solutions—can transform inefficiencies into competitive advantages, benefiting both the organization and its customers.

THE FIRST STEP TO IMPROVEMENT

The journey toward refining any work procedure begins with the critical first step: fostering awareness and acknowledgment of the need for change. This initial phase is often overlooked, as organizations may become accustomed to inefficiencies or resistant to addressing them due to the inertia of existing habits. However, without recognizing that a procedure has gaps or could be more effective, meaningful progress is impossible. Awareness serves as the foundation upon which all subsequent improvements are built, encouraging teams and stakeholders to engage in the process with clarity and purpose.

To cultivate this awareness, organizations must first adopt a mindset that views procedures as dynamic tools rather than rigid systems. This requires leaders to communicate the importance of procedural reviews as a proactive strategy for maintaining competitiveness and adaptability. A culture that values continuous improvement rather than adherence to the status quo empowers employees to voice concerns and propose changes. For example, framing process evaluations as opportunities to enhance outcomes and workflows shifts the perception from criticism to constructive development, fostering an environment where all team members feel invested in procedural success.

Gathering preliminary observations from those who interact with the procedure daily is a vital part of this step. Employees at all levels often hold valuable insights into inefficiencies but may hesitate to share them due to fear of appearing critical or uncooperative. Leaders must create channels for open dialogue, such as anonymous surveys, suggestion boxes, or feedback sessions, to capture these observations. Encouraging participation by acknowledging and acting on suggestions demonstrates that their input matters, which builds trust and engagement.

Another key aspect of this first step is identifying the specific pain points that disrupt workflows or hinder outcomes. This involves looking beyond symptoms to uncover the underlying issues that create visible inefficiencies. For instance, frequent delays in project delivery may appear to result from employee workloads, but a deeper examination might reveal poorly defined roles or misaligned priorities as the root cause. Pinpointing these pain points not only validates the need for change but also sets the stage for targeted improvements that address core problems rather than superficial symptoms.

Finally, the first step must include securing buy-in from key stakeholders who influence or oversee the procedure. Whether it's executives, department heads, or external partners, their support is essential for driving meaningful change. Engaging these stakeholders early ensures alignment on the goals of the improvement initiative and helps to overcome potential resistance. Clear communication about the benefits of addressing procedural gaps—such as increased efficiency, cost savings, or enhanced team morale—can motivate leaders to champion the process and allocate necessary resources. With awareness, collaboration, and commitment established, the foundation is set for deeper analysis and sustainable improvements.

Best practices for developing work processes

Clarity is the cornerstone of any successful work process. Without it, even the most ambitious plans or innovative strategies can falter, leading to confusion, errors, and inefficiencies. Intrinsically, clarity in work processes ensures that everyone involved understands their roles, responsibilities, and the steps needed to achieve desired outcomes. When processes are clear, teams can function with precision and confidence, minimizing miscommunication and streamlining collaboration. This foundation creates a sense of purpose and direction that anchors the entire organization.

One of the most common challenges in achieving clarity is the tendency for procedures to be overly complex or ambiguous. Overly detailed instructions can overwhelm employees, while vague guidelines leave room for interpretation, leading to inconsistent execution. A balance must be struck—processes should provide enough detail to guide action without micromanaging creativity or adaptability. For instance, instead of listing every minute step in a task, focusing on key milestones and decision points can help employees understand what's critical while leaving room for professional judgment.

Another critical component of clarity is how information is presented. Dense blocks of text or overly technical language can obscure meaning and alienate users. Instead, well-designed documentation should incorporate simplicity and accessibility. Visual aids such as flowcharts, diagrams, or step-by-step guides can significantly enhance understanding. For example, a process map that visually represents the sequence of tasks can provide employees with a quick and intuitive grasp of what needs to be done and when. Similarly, using clear, straightforward language that avoids jargon ensures that processes are comprehensible to everyone, regardless of their expertise level.

Clarity also involves consistency. Procedures should align with organizational goals and values, and every stakeholder should receive the same information about how tasks are to be executed. Inconsistent communication—where different teams or individuals operate under different interpretations of a procedure—can lead to inefficiencies and errors. This is particularly crucial in cross-functional or multinational settings, where standardized processes help bridge cultural and operational differences. Clear procedures become the common language that unites diverse teams in pursuit of shared objectives.

Achieving and maintaining clarity is an ongoing effort. Processes must be revisited and refined regularly to ensure they remain relevant and understandable as organizational needs evolve. Periodic reviews can identify areas where clarity may have eroded, such as outdated terminology or instructions that no longer align with current tools or technologies. Involving employees in these reviews ensures that the people closest to the work have a voice in shaping how it's done. By treating clarity as a dynamic, living aspect of work processes, organizations can ensure that their procedures continue to provide a solid foundation for success.

ADAPTABILITY IN AN EVOLVING WORKPLACE

In today's fast-paced and ever-changing professional landscape, adaptability has become a critical component of effective work processes. Organizations must navigate evolving technologies, shifting market demands, and an increasingly globalized workforce. Amid these changes, rigid, unyielding procedures risk becoming liabilities, stifling creativity and preventing swift responses to new challenges. By embedding adaptability into work processes, businesses can remain competitive, resilient, and innovative while fostering a culture of continuous improvement.

Adaptable processes begin with design. Traditional procedures often prioritize predictability and control, assuming a static environment. However, modern workplaces demand flexibility, requiring processes that can accommodate variability without losing their core structure. For instance, a modular approach to process design allows for individual components to be adjusted or replaced without overhauling the entire system. This method mirrors practices in agile development, where workflows are broken into manageable units that can evolve based on feedback and changing requirements, making it easier to respond to unforeseen circumstances.

Another key to adaptability lies in incorporating regular review cycles into work processes. Procedures should not be treated as one-time creations but as living systems that grow and evolve alongside the organization. Scheduled assessments—such as quarterly or annual reviews—can identify inefficiencies, account for new tools or technologies, and address changes in team dynamics or regulatory environments. For example, a logistics company might revise its routing processes annually to incorporate advancements in GPS technology or shifts in supply chain demands, ensuring efficiency even as conditions change.

The human element is also vital to adaptability. Employees are often the first to notice when a process is no longer effective or suitable. Encouraging a feedback-rich culture where team members feel empowered to suggest adjustments can uncover opportunities for improvement that might otherwise be missed. This requires leadership to be open to change, viewing deviations from established norms as opportunities for innovation rather than disruptions. Furthermore, involving employees in revising procedures fosters a sense of ownership and engagement, making transitions smoother and more effective.

Technology plays a dual role in fostering adaptability. On one hand, it drives the need for change by introducing new capabilities and tools that render old methods obsolete. On the other hand, it provides solutions that enhance flexibility. Workflow automation platforms, for instance, allow for rapid reconfiguration of tasks to accommodate changes in priorities or team composition. Similarly, data analytics tools can provide real-time insights into procedural performance, enabling organizations to make informed adjustments quickly and efficiently.

Adaptability in work processes is not just about preparing for change but embracing it as an integral part of organizational growth. By designing procedures with flexibility in mind, committing to regular reassessment, and empowering employees to contribute to their evolution, businesses can transform challenges into opportunities. This adaptability fosters resilience, ensuring that processes remain effective and aligned with goals no matter how the workplace evolves.

EFFECTIVENESS THROUGH STAKEHOLDER INVOLVEMENT

Effective work processes cannot be developed or sustained in isolation; they require the active participation of stakeholders at all levels of an organization. Stakeholder involvement ensures that processes are not only well-designed but also aligned with the goals, needs, and realities of those who use them. From senior executives to frontline employees, each perspective offers unique insights that can enhance the clarity, adaptability, and overall success of procedural design. This collaborative approach transforms processes from rigid mandates into dynamic tools that empower and unite teams.

One of the key benefits of stakeholder involvement is the alignment of processes with practical realities. Often, procedures are crafted by individuals removed from the day-to-day tasks they govern, leading to inefficiencies or gaps in execution. Involving frontline employees—those who interact most directly with the processes—ensures that workflows are grounded in actual practices and challenges. For example, in a manufacturing setting, input from line workers can reveal bottlenecks or overlooked safety concerns that designers might miss. This bottom-up insight not only improves procedural effectiveness but also fosters a sense of ownership among employees.

Stakeholder involvement also enhances buy-in and compliance. Processes imposed without consultation often face resistance, as employees may view them as irrelevant or burdensome. However, when stakeholders are part of the design and implementation process, they are more likely to understand the purpose behind the procedures and commit to following them. This collaborative approach demonstrates respect for the expertise and contributions of all team members, creating a culture where processes are seen as shared resources rather than top-down directives.

Another advantage of stakeholder involvement is its ability to foster innovation. Diverse teams bring varied perspectives, allowing for creative solutions to procedural challenges. Cross-functional collaboration, in particular, can uncover opportunities to streamline workflows and eliminate redundancies. For example, when sales, marketing, and customer support teams jointly design a client onboarding process, their combined expertise can produce a seamless experience that meets both operational and customer needs. This integration of viewpoints not only improves effectiveness but also ensures that processes are adaptable across different departments.

Leadership plays a crucial role in facilitating stakeholder involvement. Transparent communication, active listening, and an open-door policy for feedback signal that all contributions are valued. Tools such as workshops, surveys, and focus groups can be used to engage stakeholders systematically, ensuring that their voices are heard throughout the process lifecycle. Leaders must also balance diverse inputs, mediating conflicts and aligning differing priorities to create cohesive, effective workflows. This requires both empathy and decisiveness, as well as a commitment to keeping the process iterative.

By involving stakeholders at every stage—design, implementation, and refinement—organizations can ensure that work processes remain relevant, efficient, and impactful. This collaborative effort strengthens team cohesion, enhances procedural compliance, and paves the way for continuous improvement. Ultimately, the involvement of stakeholders transforms work processes from static instructions into dynamic frameworks that empower individuals and drive organizational success.

TOOLS AND TECHNOLOGIES FOR PROCEDURAL EXCELLENCE

In the pursuit of procedural excellence, tools and technologies serve as critical enablers, allowing organizations to design, implement, and refine processes with greater precision and efficiency. From basic task management platforms to sophisticated automation systems, these resources help streamline workflows, enhance communication, and ensure consistency. Leveraging the right tools not only improves the functionality of procedures but also empowers teams to adapt and innovate in response to evolving demands.

The first step in integrating technology into work processes is identifying the tools that align with organizational goals and specific procedural needs. For instance, project management software like Asana or Trello can be invaluable for tracking tasks, assigning responsibilities, and monitoring progress in collaborative environments. These platforms provide visual overviews of workflows, enabling teams to identify bottlenecks or delays in real time. Similarly, customer relationship management (CRM) systems such as Salesforce or HubSpot centralize client data and streamline sales processes, ensuring that procedures are both effective and customer-centric.

Automation technologies are another cornerstone of procedural excellence. Repetitive tasks, such as data entry or invoice processing, are prone to errors and inefficiencies when performed manually. Robotic process automation (RPA) tools like UiPath or Blue Prism can handle these tasks with speed and accuracy, freeing up human resources for more strategic work. In addition, automation can enforce procedural compliance by ensuring that steps are executed in the correct order and that necessary approvals are obtained, reducing the risk of oversight or non-compliance.

Data analytics tools also play a pivotal role in refining work processes. Platforms like Tableau or Microsoft Power BI provide actionable insights by analyzing performance metrics and identifying trends. For example, a logistics company might use analytics to pinpoint inefficiencies in delivery routes, enabling adjustments that save time and reduce costs. By continuously monitoring and analyzing procedural data, organizations can adopt a proactive approach to improvement, addressing issues before they escalate into significant challenges.

Equally important are communication and collaboration technologies, which ensure that stakeholders remain aligned and informed throughout procedural workflows. Tools such as Slack, Microsoft Teams, and Zoom facilitate real-time communication across distributed teams, breaking down silos and fostering transparency. For instance, a product development team might use a shared workspace to collaborate on design documents, hold virtual meetings, and track milestones, ensuring that everyone is working toward the same goals. These tools also enhance adaptability, as teams can quickly pivot processes in response to new information or challenges.

Tools and technologies are not a substitute for well-designed procedures but rather a complement that enhances their execution and adaptability. Selecting the right mix of platforms requires a clear understanding of organizational priorities, a willingness to invest in training, and an ongoing commitment to evaluation and refinement. By integrating technology thoughtfully and strategically, organizations can achieve procedural excellence that is not only efficient but also resilient, scalable, and aligned with their broader objectives.

ITERATIVE IMPROVEMENT AND FEEDBACK LOOPS

The most effective work processes are not static; they evolve through iterative improvement and the consistent application of feedback loops. This approach acknowledges that no procedure is perfect from the outset and that even the most well-designed workflows require regular evaluation and adjustment to remain relevant and effective. By embedding iterative improvement into the procedural lifecycle, organizations can cultivate a culture of continuous enhancement, where adaptability and learning become core strengths.

At the heart of iterative improvement lies the recognition that change is a constant in professional environments. Market dynamics, technological advancements, and organizational growth all create shifts that can render previously effective processes obsolete. An iterative mindset embraces this reality, positioning each process as a living entity that evolves through cycles of planning, execution, evaluation, and refinement. For example, in software development, agile methodologies employ sprints—short cycles that prioritize constant feedback and incremental updates—to improve both the product and the development process.

Feedback loops are essential mechanisms in this cycle, providing the data and insights needed for meaningful improvements. These loops function by collecting input at critical points in the process, analyzing the results, and using the findings to inform changes. For instance, a customer service team might monitor key performance indicators such as response time and resolution rates, then use monthly feedback reports to adjust protocols for handling support tickets. This regular influx of data ensures that changes are guided by real-world outcomes rather than assumptions or guesswork.

Incorporating diverse sources of feedback strengthens the effectiveness of iterative improvement. Employees involved in the day-to-day execution of procedures often possess valuable insights into inefficiencies or potential enhancements. Regular surveys, focus groups, or one-on-one discussions can help capture their perspectives. Similarly, feedback from external stakeholders—such as customers, vendors, or regulatory bodies—can highlight areas where processes may need adjustment to better meet expectations or compliance standards. The inclusion of varied viewpoints ensures that improvements are holistic and address the needs of all relevant parties.

Technological tools can amplify the power of feedback loops by automating data collection and analysis. Platforms like workflow management software or performance tracking systems can provide real-time metrics and visual dashboards, making it easier to spot trends and anomalies. For example, a logistics company might use tracking software to monitor delivery times and automatically flag delays, prompting a review of routing procedures. By streamlining the feedback process, these tools enable organizations to act quickly and make data-driven decisions that enhance efficiency and effectiveness.

The iterative improvement approach requires a mindset of openness and resilience within an organization. Teams must be willing to acknowledge when processes are no longer optimal and embrace change as a pathway to growth. Leaders play a crucial role in fostering this mindset by promoting transparency, encouraging experimentation, and celebrating incremental successes. When employees see that feedback leads to tangible improvements and that their input is valued, they become more engaged in the process, creating a virtuous cycle of innovation and refinement.

By prioritizing iterative improvement and embedding feedback loops into work processes, organizations can ensure that procedures remain effective, adaptable, and aligned with strategic goals. This commitment to evolution transforms processes from rigid frameworks into dynamic systems that drive success, even in the face of shifting circumstances and challenges.

Tools and technologies that support procedural excellence

In an increasingly complex and fast-paced world, technology has emerged as a cornerstone of procedural excellence, reshaping the way organizations approach their workflows and operations. Gone are the days when processes relied solely on manual effort and human oversight; today, tools and technologies serve as indispensable allies in achieving efficiency, consistency, and innovation. Whether it's managing intricate supply chains, streamlining communication in globally dispersed teams, or automating repetitive tasks, technology provides the structural foundation needed to excel in modern work environments.

One of the most significant contributions of technology lies in its ability to translate abstract procedures into tangible, actionable steps. Processes often exist as concepts on paper or as verbal instructions passed from one team to another, which can lead to gaps in understanding and execution. Digital platforms and tools bridge this divide, turning procedural designs into interactive workflows that are accessible to all relevant stakeholders. For instance, task management platforms enable teams to visualize their responsibilities, set priorities, and monitor progress in real-time, ensuring clarity and alignment across diverse functions.

Technology also addresses one of the greatest challenges in maintaining procedural excellence: adaptability. Processes that remain static risk becoming obsolete in the face of shifting market conditions, regulatory changes, or evolving customer expectations. Technological tools, designed with flexibility in mind, allow organizations to iterate and adjust their workflows seamlessly. For example, data-driven analytics platforms provide insights into performance trends, helping leaders identify when a process is underperforming or failing to meet its objectives. This capacity for dynamic adaptation ensures that procedures evolve alongside organizational needs, rather than becoming barriers to growth.

Moreover, technology plays a pivotal role in fostering collaboration and inclusivity within procedural frameworks. Modern workplaces often span continents and time zones, making effective communication a complex undertaking. Collaboration tools bridge these divides, creating virtual spaces where teams can exchange information, share updates, and resolve issues promptly. By doing so, they not only enhance the execution of procedures but also promote a culture of transparency and collective ownership. This democratization of access to information ensures that every participant, regardless of their location or role, has a voice in refining and improving workflows.

At its keystone, the integration of technology into work processes is not just about efficiency or automation; it's about empowerment. By providing individuals and teams with the right tools, organizations enable their people to focus on creative problem-solving, strategic decision-making, and meaningful contributions. Technology reduces the cognitive load associated with managing complex systems, allowing human effort to be directed toward areas where it can generate the greatest value. In doing so, it transforms procedural excellence from a distant ideal into an achievable reality, making organizations more resilient, adaptable, and innovative in the process.

TOOLS FOR WORKFLOW AND TASK MANAGEMENT

Effective workflow and task management are at the heart of procedural excellence, and the right tools can transform how individuals and teams operate. These tools provide a structured approach to organizing tasks, prioritizing goals, and tracking progress, replacing outdated methods like static spreadsheets or fragmented communication channels. By offering intuitive platforms that centralize information and responsibilities, workflow tools ensure that no task falls through the cracks, enabling teams to deliver consistent and timely results even in demanding environments.

One of the defining features of modern workflow tools is their ability to create visibility and transparency across projects. Platforms such as Asana, Trello, and Monday.com allow users to break down complex initiatives into manageable tasks while assigning responsibilities, setting deadlines, and monitoring updates in real time. This visual representation of tasks, often in the form of boards, timelines, or calendars, eliminates ambiguity and ensures alignment. For example, in a marketing campaign, a team can track content creation, approvals, and distribution seamlessly, reducing bottlenecks and ensuring timely execution.

These tools also excel at facilitating prioritization, a critical component of efficient workflows. In dynamic workplaces, tasks often compete for attention, and without clear guidance, teams can struggle to focus on what matters most. Workflow tools incorporate features like tagging, filtering, and categorization to help teams identify high-priority items quickly. With these capabilities, managers can ensure that essential tasks are tackled first, minimizing delays and maximizing resource utilization. This prioritization becomes particularly valuable during tight deadlines or when dealing with unexpected disruptions.

Collaboration is another strength of workflow and task management tools, especially in team-based environments. With built-in communication features, such as comments, file sharing, and activity logs, these platforms minimize the need for endless email chains or scattered updates. Instead, all project-related discussions and materials are centralized, making it easier for team members to stay informed and connected. Consider a software development team using a tool like Jira, where developers, designers, and testers can collaborate within a unified environment, ensuring that every stage of the project aligns with procedural objectives.

Perhaps most importantly, these tools empower teams to take ownership of their roles within a process. By providing clear task assignments and progress tracking, they foster accountability and autonomy. Team members can see how their contributions fit into the larger picture, enhancing motivation and a sense of purpose. Meanwhile, managers can monitor performance without micromanaging, relying on dashboards and reports to gain insights into productivity and potential areas for improvement. Ultimately, workflow and task management tools bridge the gap between strategy and execution, turning procedural frameworks into actionable, effective practices.

AUTOMATION FOR STREAMLINED OPERATIONS

In the quest for procedural excellence, automation has become a transformative force, reshaping how organizations approach repetitive, time-consuming tasks. By leveraging technology to handle routine processes, businesses can redirect human effort toward more strategic and creative endeavors. Automation eliminates bottlenecks, reduces errors, and accelerates workflows, making it an indispensable tool for organizations aiming to enhance efficiency and maintain a competitive edge in today's fast-paced environments.

One of the most significant advantages of automation lies in its ability to minimize human error. Tasks that require repetitive manual input, such as data entry or invoice processing, are particularly prone to mistakes when performed by people. Automation tools like robotic process automation (RPA) software can execute these functions with unmatched precision, ensuring consistency and accuracy. For instance, a financial services firm might use automation to handle payroll calculations, avoiding costly errors while freeing employees to focus on customer service and strategy.

Beyond error reduction, automation excels at speeding up processes that would otherwise consume valuable time and resources. Consider the task of onboarding new employees, which traditionally involves paperwork, data collection, and manual scheduling. With automation tools, organizations can create workflows that guide new hires through the process seamlessly—sending reminders, collecting necessary documents, and scheduling training sessions without constant oversight. This streamlining not only enhances the experience for new employees but also allows HR professionals to focus on more personalized aspects of onboarding.

Automation also plays a critical role in ensuring scalability within organizations. As businesses grow, so do their operational complexities, and manual processes can quickly become unsustainable. Automated systems are designed to handle increasing workloads without compromising performance. For example, e-commerce platforms use automation to manage inventory updates, order tracking, and customer inquiries, maintaining high levels of service even during peak demand periods. This scalability enables organizations to expand without being hindered by procedural inefficiencies.

While automation enhances efficiency, it also fosters adaptability by providing real-time insights and flexibility. Many modern automation platforms are equipped with analytics capabilities, allowing organizations to monitor process performance and identify areas for improvement. If an automated process begins to underperform, adjustments can be made swiftly, ensuring continued alignment with organizational goals. This iterative approach to improvement demonstrates that automation is not a static solution but a dynamic tool that evolves alongside an organization's needs.

Primarily, automation is not about replacing humans but empowering them to work smarter. By offloading mundane and repetitive tasks, employees can dedicate their energy to activities that require empathy, critical thinking, and innovation. When implemented thoughtfully, automation becomes a collaborative partner in achieving procedural excellence, enhancing both the efficiency of operations and the quality of outcomes. This harmonious blend of technology and human ingenuity underscores why automation has become a cornerstone of modern workflow optimization.

DATA ANALYTICS FOR PROCEDURAL INSIGHTS

In the modern era, data has become the lifeblood of organizational success, offering unparalleled opportunities to refine work processes and achieve procedural excellence. Data analytics tools provide a clear window into how processes function, revealing inefficiencies, strengths, and areas ripe for improvement. By leveraging analytics, organizations can move beyond intuition and guesswork, using evidence-based insights to make informed decisions that enhance operational effectiveness and long-term resilience.

The primary value of data analytics lies in its ability to uncover patterns and trends that are invisible through traditional observation. Every process generates data points, from task completion times to resource utilization rates. Analytical tools compile and interpret these data streams, offering a granular view of procedural performance. For instance, a manufacturing company might analyze production data to identify bottlenecks in its assembly line, allowing it to address specific delays and optimize workflow without unnecessary trial and error.

Real-time monitoring is another key strength of data analytics. Many platforms are designed to track processes as they unfold, providing immediate feedback on performance metrics. This capability is invaluable in fast-paced environments where delays or errors can cascade into significant disruptions. A logistics company, for example, can use real-time analytics to monitor its supply chain, identifying late shipments or inventory shortages before they escalate into larger problems. This proactive approach ensures that processes remain aligned with organizational goals and customer expectations.

Beyond identifying inefficiencies, data analytics empowers organizations to predict and prepare for future challenges. Predictive analytics, fueled by machine learning and artificial intelligence, can forecast potential disruptions or resource demands based on historical data. In a healthcare setting, for instance, predictive tools might analyze patient intake patterns to anticipate staffing needs, ensuring that the hospital remains adequately resourced during peak periods. This forward-looking approach transforms procedural management from reactive problem-solving into strategic foresight.

Moreover, data analytics fosters a culture of accountability and continuous improvement. When procedural performance is measured and shared transparently, it encourages individuals and teams to take ownership of their contributions. Dashboards and reports make it easy to track progress against key performance indicators (KPIs), offering both motivation and clarity. Teams can celebrate successes when goals are met and collaborate on solutions when challenges arise, creating a cycle of ongoing refinement.

Fundamentally, the power of data analytics lies in its ability to translate complexity into clarity. By turning raw data into actionable insights, organizations can understand the true dynamics of their processes and make decisions that drive meaningful change. When used strategically, analytics becomes more than a tool—it becomes a guiding compass, ensuring that work procedures are not only efficient but also adaptive, sustainable, and aligned with broader organizational objectives.

COMMUNICATION AND COLLABORATION TECHNOLOGIES

1. In the realm of procedural excellence, effective communication and collaboration are fundamental. Without seamless interaction between team members, stakeholders, and departments, even the most well-designed processes can falter. Communication and collaboration technologies play a pivotal role in bridging gaps, enhancing transparency, and ensuring that everyone involved in a process works cohesively toward shared goals. These tools have evolved far beyond basic messaging systems, now offering integrated solutions that transform how organizations operate.

Modern collaboration platforms, such as Microsoft Teams, Slack, and Zoom, enable real-time communication across geographic and organizational boundaries. These tools consolidate messaging, video conferencing, and file sharing into unified systems, eliminating the inefficiencies of scattered communication channels. For example, during a product launch, marketing, sales, and development teams can coordinate seamlessly through these platforms, ensuring that updates are shared instantly and that feedback loops remain uninterrupted. This level of connectivity prevents misunderstandings, accelerates decision-making, and keeps teams aligned.

In addition to fostering direct communication, collaboration technologies provide a framework for centralized knowledge management. Tools like Confluence or Google Workspace allow teams to document procedures, store critical resources, and create accessible repositories of institutional knowledge. These centralized hubs ensure that everyone has access to up-to-date information, reducing reliance on verbal instructions or siloed expertise. For instance, a customer service team can refer to a shared database of solutions and protocols, ensuring consistent responses across representatives. This not only improves efficiency but also enhances the quality of service.

Collaboration technologies are also instrumental in enabling asynchronous workflows, a critical advantage in today's increasingly remote and globalized work environments. Tools like Miro, Trello, and Notion allow teams to contribute to projects on their own schedules, offering updates and completing tasks without the need for constant overlap in working hours. This flexibility is particularly valuable in multinational organizations, where time zone differences can present challenges. Asynchronous collaboration ensures that progress continues uninterrupted, regardless of when or where team members are working.

Perhaps one of the most transformative aspects of these technologies is their capacity to integrate with other procedural tools, such as workflow automation and data analytics platforms. For example, Slack can be linked to project management tools like Asana or Jira, creating automated notifications for task updates or deadlines. This integration streamlines operations by reducing manual updates and keeping all stakeholders informed without additional effort. Such interconnected systems enhance procedural transparency and create a cohesive ecosystem where technology supports every aspect of communication and collaboration.

At its base, communication and collaboration technologies empower organizations to work smarter, not harder. By fostering connectivity, knowledge sharing, and integration, they enable teams to overcome the barriers that often hinder procedural success. When these tools are thoughtfully implemented, they become not just facilitators of daily operations but drivers of innovation, ensuring that every voice is heard and every effort is aligned with broader organizational goals. Through these technologies, businesses can achieve the synergy necessary to turn efficient processes into exceptional outcomes.

TAILORING TOOLS TO ORGANIZATIONAL NEEDS

No two organizations are alike, and this fundamental truth underscores the importance of tailoring tools and technologies to fit specific procedural needs. While a wide array of platforms and solutions exists to support procedural excellence, their effectiveness depends on how well they align with an organization's structure, culture, and objectives. Adopting the wrong tools can create inefficiencies rather than resolve them, making it essential to select, adapt, and implement technologies thoughtfully and strategically.

The first step in tailoring tools is conducting a thorough needs assessment. This process involves understanding the unique challenges and goals of the organization and identifying gaps in existing workflows. For instance, a manufacturing company seeking to streamline its supply chain might prioritize tools that enhance inventory tracking and vendor communication. In contrast, a creative agency might need collaboration platforms that facilitate idea-sharing and client feedback. By focusing on specific pain points, organizations can ensure that the tools they adopt directly address their procedural priorities rather than introducing unnecessary complexity.

Another key consideration is scalability. The tools selected should not only meet current needs but also adapt as the organization evolves. For startups and small businesses, this means choosing technologies that grow with the company, avoiding costly transitions to new platforms as operations expand. Larger organizations, on the other hand, may need tools that integrate seamlessly across multiple departments or global locations. Cloud-based solutions, for example, offer scalability and flexibility, allowing organizations to add features or users without significant disruptions to existing processes.

Customization is another vital factor in tailoring tools to organizational needs. Many technologies offer configurable features, enabling businesses to adjust workflows, interfaces, and functionalities to suit their specific requirements. For instance, customer relationship management (CRM) systems like Salesforce allow users to design custom dashboards and reports, ensuring that employees at different levels of the organization receive the information most relevant to their roles. Similarly, enterprise resource planning (ERP) systems can be adapted to reflect an organization's unique supply chain or financial processes, ensuring alignment with strategic objectives.

The success of any tool also hinges on user adoption, which requires careful consideration of the organization's culture and employee capabilities. Even the most sophisticated technology will fail if employees find it difficult to use or perceive it as a burden. To address this, organizations should involve end-users in the selection and implementation process, gathering feedback and ensuring that the chosen tools are intuitive and accessible. Comprehensive training and ongoing support are equally important, fostering confidence and competence among users. By prioritizing usability and engagement, organizations can maximize the value of their technological investments.

Organizations must continually evaluate and refine their toolsets to ensure sustained alignment with their needs. Regularly reviewing how technologies perform in practice allows for adjustments and upgrades that keep pace with industry trends and internal changes. For example, a company that initially adopts a basic project management tool might later integrate advanced analytics capabilities as its procedural goals shift toward data-driven decision-making. This iterative approach ensures that tools remain relevant and effective, contributing to long-term procedural excellence.

Tailoring tools to organizational needs is not a one-size-fits-all endeavor but a dynamic process requiring attention to detail, flexibility, and a deep understanding of operational goals. When done effectively, it transforms technology from a mere utility into a strategic asset, enabling organizations to achieve clarity, adaptability, and efficiency in their processes. By selecting and customizing tools with purpose, businesses can create systems that empower employees, streamline workflows, and drive meaningful results.

The Role of Communication and Collaboration

Work procedures are often hailed as the backbone of organizational success, offering clarity and efficiency. However, even the most well-designed processes can fail spectacularly if the people responsible for executing them are not genuinely invested in their success. This investment, or "buy-in," is more than mere compliance; it's an alignment of understanding, belief, and willingness among team members. When buy-in is absent, even the most promising initiatives can encounter resistance, stagnation, or outright rejection. Without the support and enthusiasm of those involved, a process, no matter how sophisticated, risks becoming an administrative burden rather than a tool for progress.

The consequences of ignoring buy-in can be both immediate and long-lasting. In the short term, teams may drag their feet, produce subpar results, or develop workarounds that undermine the intended outcomes of a new procedure. Over time, this resistance can erode trust in leadership and create a culture of disengagement. When employees perceive processes as top-down mandates imposed without their input, they become less likely to engage wholeheartedly in other organizational initiatives. This disengagement is not just an inconvenience; it can lead to higher turnover, lower productivity, and a stagnation of innovation across the board.

Consider the example of a multinational corporation that introduced a new project management software to streamline cross-functional collaboration. Despite the tool's potential, its implementation floundered. Employees resisted its use, citing a lack of training and unclear benefits. Managers struggled to enforce compliance, and within six months, the software was abandoned. This failure was not due to the software's inadequacies but to the lack of transparency and involvement during its introduction. Had the organization taken the time to secure buy-in by involving key stakeholders and clearly communicating the software's value, the outcome could have been drastically different.

At the heart of the issue is a common misstep: the assumption that people will automatically support changes simply because they are logical or beneficial. Leaders often underestimate the emotional and psychological hurdles that accompany change. People need to feel included and respected in decisions that affect their daily work. When they don't, resistance often manifests as skepticism, avoidance, or outright defiance. This is particularly true when changes are abrupt, inadequately explained, or perceived as disruptive rather than empowering.

Buy-in, therefore, is not a luxury but a necessity. Securing it requires thoughtful planning, clear communication, and genuine collaboration. It involves understanding the perspectives of those who will implement the process and addressing their concerns proactively. By fostering a sense of ownership and demonstrating transparency, leaders can transform potential resistance into active support. The journey to successful buy-in may require extra effort upfront, but the rewards—loyalty, enthusiasm, and sustainable adoption of processes—are well worth it.

THE ANATOMY OF RESISTANCE

Resistance to new work procedures is a natural human response, rooted in psychology and organizational dynamics. At its core principle, resistance arises from fear of the unknown, disruption of established routines, and a lack of trust in leadership or the proposed changes. To understand why procedures often fail despite their logical or practical merits, it is essential to dissect the underlying causes of this resistance. By addressing these root issues, organizations can anticipate challenges and navigate the delicate process of securing genuine support from their teams.

One of the primary drivers of resistance is a perceived threat to autonomy. When new procedures are introduced without consulting the individuals who will implement them, employees often feel disempowered. This sense of exclusion can lead to a phenomenon known as "ownership bias," where people reject ideas or changes they perceive as being imposed upon them. In the workplace, this often manifests as passive resistance—employees may comply superficially but fail to engage fully, thereby undermining the procedure's effectiveness.

Another significant factor is the discomfort of change itself. Change, even when beneficial, requires individuals to adapt, learn new skills, and abandon familiar routines. This adaptation often triggers "change fatigue," particularly in organizations that frequently introduce new systems without sufficient support or follow-through. Employees facing a constant barrage of updates may view new procedures as yet another transient initiative, unworthy of their time and energy. This skepticism grows stronger when past changes have been poorly managed or abandoned midway, reinforcing a cycle of mistrust.

Resistance can also stem from a lack of clarity about the purpose and benefits of a new procedure. If the "why" behind a change is not effectively communicated, employees may struggle to see how the new approach aligns with their goals or the organization's broader objectives. This lack of alignment creates a disconnect, where employees see the procedure as irrelevant, overly bureaucratic, or a hindrance to their productivity. For example, a quality assurance team tasked with following new compliance guidelines might resist if they view the guidelines as slowing their workflow rather than ensuring product safety.

Interpersonal dynamics within the workplace can further amplify resistance. Teams often mirror the attitudes of influential members or leaders. If a vocal manager expresses doubts about the viability of a new procedure, their skepticism can ripple through the team, intensifying resistance. Conversely, when leadership openly embraces and champions a change, it can mitigate doubts and foster acceptance. Recognizing the social aspects of resistance is crucial, as resistance is rarely an individual phenomenon; it is often a collective response influenced by group dynamics and organizational culture.

To address resistance effectively, organizations must go beyond treating it as an obstacle to overcome and instead view it as valuable feedback. Resistance often signals deeper issues—such as unmet needs, unaddressed concerns, or misaligned priorities—that deserve attention. By involving employees early in the process, listening to their concerns, and demonstrating a willingness to adapt, leaders can transform resistance into collaboration. Understanding the anatomy of resistance is not just about diagnosing the problem; it is about building a foundation of trust, transparency, and shared commitment to success.

Transparency as a Cornerstone

Transparency is the bedrock of successful procedural adoption. Without it, even the most well-designed systems are prone to skepticism, resistance, and eventual failure. Transparency ensures that employees understand not only the mechanics of a new procedure but also its rationale, anticipated benefits, and potential challenges. By cultivating open communication and trust, organizations can create an environment where employees feel informed, respected, and aligned with the direction of change.

The importance of transparency begins with explaining the *why* behind a procedure. People are far more likely to embrace change when they understand its purpose and relevance. For instance, a company introducing a new quality control process might highlight how it will reduce product recalls, improve customer satisfaction, and enhance the organization's reputation. Without this clarity, employees may perceive the new procedure as unnecessary micromanagement or an added burden. Transparency bridges this gap by linking the procedure to tangible outcomes that resonate with both organizational goals and individual roles.

Equally critical is addressing the *how*—the details of implementation and expected results. Employees need to see a roadmap that outlines what the procedure involves, how it will impact their daily work, and what support will be provided during the transition. Ambiguity breeds confusion and frustration, often leading to resistance. In contrast, a transparent approach might involve sharing detailed rollout plans, timelines, and metrics for success. For example, a transparent communication plan could include team meetings to introduce the procedure, Q&A sessions to address concerns, and regular updates on its progress and results.

Transparency also involves acknowledging potential challenges and limitations. No procedure is flawless, and employees are more likely to trust leaders who demonstrate honesty about the risks or difficulties involved. This honesty fosters credibility, showing that leadership has thoroughly considered the change and is prepared to address setbacks. For instance, an organization adopting a new workflow system might admit upfront that there could be a learning curve, while simultaneously outlining the training resources and support available to ease the transition. Such candor helps employees feel prepared and supported, rather than blindsided.

A key aspect of transparency is inviting feedback and encouraging dialogue throughout the process. When employees have opportunities to voice their concerns, ask questions, and offer suggestions, they feel valued and included in the decision-making process. This sense of inclusion can dramatically increase buy-in. For example, a multinational company implementing standardized procedures across diverse teams might host regional focus groups to gather input on how cultural or operational nuances could be accommodated. By incorporating this feedback, the organization not only improves the procedure but also reinforces a culture of mutual respect and collaboration.

Ultimately, transparency is not a one-time effort but an ongoing commitment to open and honest communication. It extends beyond the initial rollout of a procedure, encompassing regular updates on progress, adjustments based on feedback, and recognition of employee contributions. When transparency becomes a cornerstone of procedural design and implementation, it transforms work processes from mandates into collaborative efforts. This shift builds trust, empowers employees, and lays the foundation for sustained success in any organizational initiative.

THE ROLE OF TEAM INVOLVEMENT

Effective work procedures do not exist in isolation—they thrive when shaped by the input and collaboration of the people who will implement them. Team involvement is more than a gesture of inclusion; it is a critical factor in ensuring that processes are both practical and sustainable. When employees are active participants in the design, refinement, and execution of work procedures, they develop a sense of ownership that transforms potential resistance into commitment. By valuing their insights and fostering collaboration, organizations create processes that not only align with strategic goals but also resonate with those on the front lines of execution.

At its focal point, team involvement builds ownership. Employees who are included in discussions about procedures are more likely to view them as *their* processes, not as top-down mandates. This sense of ownership creates intrinsic motivation to see the procedures succeed. For example, a manufacturing team tasked with improving quality control is far more likely to adopt new protocols if they have contributed to identifying inefficiencies and brainstorming solutions. Their involvement ensures that the resulting procedure is both realistic and reflective of their expertise, reducing the likelihood of resistance or noncompliance.

Team involvement also enhances the quality of the procedures themselves. Employees who perform tasks daily often have nuanced insights into what works and what doesn't. Their practical knowledge can uncover inefficiencies, bottlenecks, or unintended consequences that might escape higher-level planners. For instance, a customer service team might highlight how a proposed script protocol could inadvertently frustrate clients, leading to modifications that balance standardization with empathy. By tapping into this firsthand experience, organizations can design procedures that are not only efficient but also adaptable to real-world scenarios.

Involving teams in the process fosters collaboration and strengthens workplace relationships. When employees feel that their voices are heard, they are more likely to trust leadership and engage constructively with colleagues. This collaboration is particularly vital in cross-functional or multinational teams, where diverse perspectives can enrich procedural design. For example, when a global company seeks to standardize its supply chain processes, engaging representatives from regional offices ensures that local challenges and cultural nuances are considered. The result is a unified procedure that respects diversity while maintaining consistency.

Team involvement is a powerful tool for change management. Change, even when necessary, is often met with apprehension. By involving teams early in the process, organizations can address concerns proactively and build a coalition of advocates who champion the change. These advocates, often referred to as "change champions," serve as liaisons between leadership and their peers, helping to disseminate information, answer questions, and generate enthusiasm for the new procedure. For example, in an IT rollout, team members who have participated in beta testing can share their positive experiences, reducing anxiety and encouraging adoption among their colleagues.

The benefits of team involvement extend far beyond the immediate success of a procedure. It cultivates a culture of trust, accountability, and continuous improvement, where employees feel empowered to contribute to the organization's growth. By prioritizing collaboration and inclusivity, leaders not only enhance procedural outcomes but also reinforce the idea that every employee plays a vital role in shaping the future of the workplace. In doing so, they transform processes from static directives into dynamic frameworks for innovation and success.

Practical Insights for Achieving Buy-In

Securing buy-in for new work procedures requires more than a well-structured plan; it demands deliberate and strategic efforts to align employees' perceptions, motivations, and trust in the proposed changes. Achieving this alignment involves blending communication, collaboration, and reinforcement into a cohesive strategy that addresses the needs and concerns of the team. By adopting practical, actionable approaches, leaders can pave the way for smoother implementation and sustained commitment to new processes.

The first step in achieving buy-in is clear and tailored communication. A one-size-fits-all announcement rarely suffices; instead, messages should be customized for different audiences within the organization. Leaders should articulate the purpose, benefits, and implications of the procedure in terms that resonate with each group. For instance, frontline employees might need to understand how the process improves their day-to-day efficiency, while executives might focus on cost savings or compliance benefits. Using multiple channels—meetings, emails, infographics, or videos—can further ensure that the message is both accessible and memorable, catering to varied preferences for absorbing information.

Another critical insight is the value of early involvement. Engaging employees during the planning and design phases not only fosters a sense of ownership but also surfaces potential challenges before they escalate. Organizations can create focus groups, hold brainstorming sessions, or conduct surveys to gather input on the procedure's design and implementation. For example, a hospital implementing a new patient intake system might involve nurses, administrative staff, and physicians in initial discussions to ensure the system is practical for all users. This proactive approach not only improves the process itself but also signals to employees that their expertise and opinions are valued.

Demonstrating leadership support is equally vital. Employees are more likely to embrace a new procedure when they see leaders actively championing it. This advocacy goes beyond verbal endorsements; it includes visible participation and accountability. For instance, if a company introduces a new project management tool, managers and executives should model its use in their own workflows, showing that the procedure is not just for lower-level staff but applies universally. Such actions reinforce the legitimacy of the change and build trust by proving that leaders are willing to adapt alongside their teams.

Training and resources play a pivotal role in overcoming apprehension and enabling employees to succeed with new processes. Resistance often stems from a lack of confidence in one's ability to adapt. Comprehensive training programs, paired with accessible resources like step-by-step guides or helplines, can bridge this gap. For example, an organization rolling out a new software system might offer interactive workshops, online tutorials, and ongoing support to ensure employees feel equipped to navigate the change. When employees feel prepared, they are more likely to approach the procedure with enthusiasm rather than apprehension.

Ongoing feedback and recognition are essential for sustaining buy-in over time. Procedures should not be static; they must evolve based on user experiences and shifting needs. Regular check-ins, anonymous surveys, or feedback platforms can help organizations identify what's working and what needs adjustment. Moreover, recognizing and celebrating early adopters and success stories can boost morale and reinforce commitment.

For instance, highlighting a team that has achieved measurable improvements through a new procedure can inspire others to follow suit, creating a ripple effect of positivity and engagement.

Achieving buy-in is a dynamic process that requires intentionality at every stage, from planning to post-implementation. By focusing on clear communication, early involvement, visible leadership, adequate training, and continuous feedback, organizations can transform resistance into cooperation and skepticism into enthusiasm. These practical strategies not only enhance procedural adoption but also build a culture of trust and collaboration, ensuring that future changes are met with open minds and willing hands.

A SHARED PATH TO SUCCESS

The successful implementation of any work procedure is not a solitary endeavor—it is a collective journey that thrives on unity, trust, and mutual commitment. A shared path to success requires leaders and employees to align their goals, collaborate effectively, and embrace a culture of partnership. When all stakeholders view the procedure not as a top-down directive but as a shared effort toward a common objective, the likelihood of long-term success dramatically increases.

One of the most critical components of this shared journey is aligning individual and organizational goals. Employees are more likely to embrace a procedure when they see how it benefits not only the company but also their personal or professional growth. For example, a new performance management system designed to improve efficiency should also emphasize how it supports employees' career development, such as by providing clearer feedback or identifying opportunities for skill enhancement. By framing procedures as tools that serve everyone's interests, organizations can foster a sense of collective investment in their success.

Trust forms the foundation of a shared path to success. Without trust in leadership, the procedure itself, or the process of its implementation, employees may remain skeptical or disengaged. Building this trust begins with transparency, as discussed earlier, but also requires consistency in actions and messaging. Leaders who involve employees in decision-making, deliver on promises, and remain approachable throughout the implementation process create an environment where trust flourishes. For instance, a team leader who acknowledges challenges, listens to concerns, and provides timely updates demonstrates reliability, which inspires confidence and cooperation among team members.

Collaboration is another vital element of a shared path. Effective collaboration ensures that procedures are not imposed but co-created, leveraging the collective expertise and creativity of the workforce. Cross-functional teams, task forces, or committees dedicated to procedural refinement can break down silos and foster a sense of shared responsibility. For example, a retail company seeking to streamline inventory management might form a team comprising store employees, supply chain experts, and IT professionals to ensure the procedure is both practical and technologically sound. This inclusive approach ensures that diverse perspectives are considered and that the procedure works across all levels of the organization.

Celebrating milestones and recognizing contributions along the way reinforces the sense of a shared journey. Procedural implementation is often a long process that requires sustained effort, and acknowledging progress can boost morale and maintain momentum. Whether it's a company-wide announcement celebrating early wins, a small thank-you to a team that went above and beyond, or recognition for employees who have championed the procedure, these gestures create a culture of appreciation. Such recognition reminds everyone that success is a collective achievement and encourages continued collaboration.

Ultimately, a shared path to success transforms the narrative around work procedures. Instead of being seen as rigid, burdensome mandates, procedures become dynamic frameworks for achieving common goals. When organizations prioritize alignment, trust, collaboration, and recognition, they create a culture where employees feel empowered to contribute to and benefit from the success of new initiatives. In this way, work procedures evolve into catalysts for innovation, cohesion, and growth—reflecting the true potential of what a united workforce can achieve.

Using Communication to Align Diverse Stakeholders in Multinational or Cross-Functional Settings

In an increasingly interconnected world, aligning diverse stakeholders has become both a necessity and a formidable challenge. Whether within multinational corporations or cross-functional teams, stakeholders often bring unique perspectives shaped by their cultural, professional, and organizational backgrounds. These differences, while enriching, can also create friction when attempting to implement standardized work procedures. The key to overcoming these challenges lies in understanding the inherent complexity of diverse stakeholders and harnessing it as a strength rather than a limitation.

At the heart of this complexity is the diversity of goals and priorities among stakeholders. A marketing department might prioritize creativity and brand consistency, while a finance team might focus on cost efficiency and risk management. In a multinational setting, regional managers may prioritize local market needs over global strategies. These conflicting priorities can make achieving consensus on procedural changes seem daunting. However, recognizing and addressing these disparities is essential for crafting procedures that balance varying objectives while aligning with the organization's overarching vision.

Cultural differences further complicate stakeholder dynamics. In multinational teams, variations in communication styles, decision-making approaches, and attitudes toward hierarchy can lead to misunderstandings or unintentional exclusion. For instance, in cultures that value indirect communication, overly direct feedback may be perceived as abrasive. Conversely, in cultures that prize assertiveness, subtle hints may be overlooked entirely. These differences can hinder collaboration unless explicitly acknowledged and bridged through thoughtful communication strategies.

Geographical dispersion adds another layer of complexity. Teams spread across time zones face logistical challenges, such as coordinating meetings or ensuring equal access to information. Remote work environments, increasingly common in globalized organizations, can exacerbate these issues by creating physical and psychological distance. Without deliberate efforts to maintain consistent communication, stakeholders may feel disconnected, leading to disengagement or misalignment in procedural implementation.

Finally, power dynamics within cross-functional or multinational teams can influence the level of participation and buy-in from stakeholders. Senior leaders may dominate discussions, leaving junior team members hesitant to voice concerns. Similarly, regional offices might feel overshadowed by corporate headquarters, creating a sense of exclusion or resistance. These dynamics, if unaddressed, can result in a lack of commitment to new procedures, undermining their effectiveness.

Understanding the complexity of diverse stakeholders is the first step toward alignment. By recognizing the unique challenges posed by differing priorities, cultural norms, geographical barriers, and power dynamics, organizations can craft strategies that foster inclusivity and collaboration. In this complexity lies an opportunity: to build procedures that are not only efficient but also reflective of the collective wisdom and strengths of a diverse workforce. When approached thoughtfully, the alignment of diverse stakeholders becomes a powerful driver of innovation, cohesion, and success.

IDENTIFYING BARRIERS TO EFFECTIVE COMMUNICATION

Effective communication is the backbone of aligning diverse stakeholders, yet it is often obstructed by a range of barriers that can derail even the best-intentioned initiatives. To navigate these obstacles, organizations must first recognize the factors that impede communication within multinational or cross-functional teams. By identifying and addressing these barriers, leaders can foster clarity, inclusivity, and collaboration, ensuring that work procedures are implemented successfully.

One of the most pervasive barriers is language. In multinational settings, stakeholders often speak different native languages, and even when a common language, such as English, is used, varying levels of proficiency can lead to misunderstandings. Subtle differences in word choice, phrasing, or tone might result in unintentional miscommunication. For example, a phrase intended as constructive feedback might be perceived as overly critical or dismissive due to cultural differences in how directness is expressed. This linguistic disconnect can create confusion, frustration, and a lack of alignment among team members.

Cultural norms further complicate communication. Different cultures have unique approaches to conveying ideas, making decisions, and resolving conflicts. In some cultures, hierarchical communication is the norm, where employees defer to senior leaders for guidance. In others, egalitarian approaches encourage open dialogue regardless of rank. When these norms clash, they can create tension or inhibit the free exchange of ideas. For instance, a manager from a culture that values consensus may misinterpret the silence of stakeholders from a hierarchy-driven culture as agreement rather than deference, leading to misaligned expectations.

Geographical dispersion and time zone differences also present significant hurdles. Remote teams often struggle with scheduling meetings at times convenient for all participants, resulting in uneven engagement. Stakeholders located in different regions may also have limited access to the same information, creating disparities in understanding and participation. Furthermore, digital communication tools, while useful, can sometimes exacerbate the problem by reducing opportunities for nuanced, face-to-face interactions that help build rapport and trust.

Organizational silos, common in cross-functional settings, add another layer of complexity. Teams within different departments often develop their own terminologies, priorities, and workflows, which can lead to misunderstandings when collaborating on shared procedures. For instance, an IT team might emphasize technical feasibility, while a sales team prioritizes customer experience. Without deliberate efforts to bridge these gaps, communication can become fragmented, hindering alignment and mutual understanding.

Lastly, psychological barriers such as fear of judgment, perceived power imbalances, or resistance to change can stifle communication. Stakeholders may hesitate to share concerns or ideas if they feel their input will be dismissed or judged harshly. This reluctance can result in a lack of feedback during critical stages of procedural development, leaving potential issues unaddressed until they escalate into larger problems.

Identifying these barriers is crucial for crafting communication strategies that are both inclusive and effective. By acknowledging linguistic challenges, respecting cultural differences, addressing geographical and organizational divides, and creating a psychologically safe environment, leaders can mitigate the risks of miscommunication. Overcoming these barriers requires intentionality, adaptability, and a commitment to fostering connections across diverse teams—an effort that ultimately strengthens alignment and ensures the success of any initiative.

STRATEGIES FOR BUILDING A UNIFIED VISION

Creating a unified vision is essential for aligning diverse stakeholders, especially in multinational or cross-functional settings where competing priorities and varied perspectives can hinder collaboration. A unified vision serves as a guiding framework, ensuring that all parties understand and commit to the overarching goals of a procedure. To achieve this alignment, organizations must implement deliberate strategies that foster clarity, inclusivity, and collective ownership.

The first step in building a unified vision is crafting a clear and compelling purpose statement. This statement should articulate why the work procedure is necessary, what it aims to achieve, and how it aligns with the broader objectives of the organization. By focusing on the "why," leaders can engage stakeholders on a deeper, more emotional level. For example, rather than framing a procedural change as a way to cut costs, it can be presented as an opportunity to enhance customer satisfaction or improve team efficiency—benefits that resonate universally.

Early engagement of stakeholders is another critical strategy. Inviting representatives from various teams, regions, or functional areas to participate in the planning and design phases ensures that the vision reflects diverse perspectives. This inclusivity not only improves the relevance of the procedure but also fosters a sense of ownership among participants. For instance, an international corporation implementing a new supply chain protocol might involve both on-the-ground logistics teams and senior management in its development, ensuring that the procedure is practical and aligned with strategic goals.

Visual tools and narratives can also play a powerful role in unifying stakeholders. Visual aids like roadmaps, flowcharts, or infographics can simplify complex processes and make them more accessible to a wide audience. Complementing these tools with stories or examples that illustrate the benefits of the procedure helps stakeholders relate to the vision on a personal level. For instance, sharing a story about how a similar procedure improved operations in another department or location can inspire confidence and excitement about the change.

Facilitating alignment workshops or vision-building sessions provides a structured environment for stakeholders to collaborate and contribute to the shared vision. These sessions can include activities like goal-setting exercises, role-playing scenarios, or discussions to address potential challenges. The emphasis should be on creating a space where all voices are heard and differences are reconciled. Such workshops not only clarify the vision but also build trust and camaraderie among stakeholders, laying a solid foundation for future collaboration.

Consistency in communication reinforces and sustains the unified vision throughout the implementation process. Leaders must ensure that the core message remains consistent across all channels and touchpoints, from email updates and team meetings to one-on-one conversations. Mixed messages or shifting priorities can erode trust and undermine alignment. Additionally, reinforcing the vision through storytelling, data, and regular progress updates keeps stakeholders engaged and motivated.

By combining clarity, inclusivity, and consistent communication, organizations can build a unified vision that transcends individual differences and aligns diverse stakeholders. This vision serves as a north star, guiding all participants through the complexities of procedural implementation and fostering a collective sense of purpose. When stakeholders feel connected to the "big picture," they are more likely to collaborate effectively and contribute to the long-term success of the initiative.

LEVERAGING TOOLS AND TECHNOLOGIES

In today's interconnected and technology-driven world, tools and technologies are indispensable for aligning diverse stakeholders. Whether managing multinational teams spread across time zones or integrating cross-functional groups with varied expertise, the right technological solutions can bridge communication gaps, enhance collaboration, and ensure procedural success. However, leveraging these tools effectively requires careful selection, thoughtful implementation, and a commitment to fostering digital inclusivity.

Collaboration platforms form the backbone of stakeholder communication in complex settings. Tools like Microsoft Teams, Slack, and Zoom enable real-time interactions, file sharing, and task management, fostering seamless collaboration across geographical boundaries. For instance, using video conferencing for regular check-ins allows stakeholders from different regions or departments to engage in meaningful discussions, breaking down silos. These platforms also offer asynchronous communication options, such as message threads or recorded updates, ensuring that team members in different time zones can stay informed without disrupting their schedules.

Project management tools, such as Asana, Trello, and Jira, are equally critical for maintaining alignment throughout procedural development and implementation. These tools provide a centralized space for tracking tasks, assigning responsibilities, and monitoring progress. Visual features like Kanban boards or Gantt charts make complex workflows more accessible, helping stakeholders understand how their contributions fit into the larger process. By offering transparency and accountability, project management tools reduce the risk of miscommunication and ensure that all parties remain aligned.

Knowledge-sharing platforms play a vital role in ensuring that stakeholders have access to the information they need. Centralized repositories like SharePoint, Confluence, or Google Drive allow teams to store and organize documents, procedural guidelines, and updates in a structured manner. These tools are particularly useful for maintaining consistency in multinational or cross-functional settings, where stakeholders might otherwise rely on fragmented or outdated information. Features such as version control and collaborative editing ensure that everyone works with the most accurate and up-to-date resources.

Advanced technologies, such as AI-powered analytics and automated workflows, can further enhance alignment by streamlining processes and providing actionable insights. AI tools can analyze data from stakeholder interactions to identify potential areas of misalignment or conflict, enabling proactive resolution. Automation tools, such as Zapier or Power Automate, reduce manual effort by integrating different software systems and creating workflows that handle repetitive tasks, freeing up stakeholders to focus on strategic priorities.

While these tools offer significant advantages, their effectiveness depends on thoughtful implementation and user adoption. Training sessions and onboarding materials are essential for ensuring that all stakeholders, regardless of their technical expertise, can use the tools confidently. Additionally, leaders must prioritize inclusivity by selecting platforms that accommodate diverse needs, such as multilingual interfaces or accessibility features for individuals with disabilities. A one-size-fits-all approach can alienate stakeholders and hinder collaboration, so customization and user feedback should guide the selection and deployment of tools.

In leveraging tools and technologies, the goal is not merely to adopt the latest software but to create an ecosystem that supports alignment and collaboration. By investing in the right platforms, organizations can overcome logistical and cultural barriers, foster transparency, and enable stakeholders to work toward shared objectives efficiently. When used thoughtfully, technology becomes not just a facilitator but a unifying force, driving the success of complex procedural initiatives.

ADAPTING COMMUNICATION STYLES FOR INCLUSIVITY

Inclusivity in communication is crucial when working with diverse stakeholders, especially in multinational or cross-functional settings. Differences in culture, language, hierarchy, and professional expertise can create communication gaps, misunderstandings, or even resentment. To align stakeholders effectively, leaders must adapt their communication styles to ensure that every individual feels heard, respected, and valued. Inclusivity is not merely a courtesy; it is a strategic necessity for fostering collaboration and achieving shared objectives.

One key aspect of inclusive communication is cultural sensitivity. Stakeholders from different cultural backgrounds often have distinct communication norms. For instance, some cultures prioritize direct, assertive communication, while others value subtlety and indirect expressions. Leaders must learn to navigate these differences by balancing clarity with respect for diverse preferences. Asking open-ended questions, listening actively, and avoiding assumptions are foundational practices that demonstrate cultural awareness and encourage genuine dialogue.

Language is another critical factor in inclusive communication. In multinational teams, using a shared language—often English—can create barriers for non-native speakers. To address this, communicators should aim for simplicity, avoiding idiomatic expressions, jargon, or complex sentence structures that may be confusing. Additionally, incorporating tools like real-time translation software or multilingual resources can enhance accessibility. Offering written summaries after meetings or discussions ensures that stakeholders have a reference point, reducing the risk of misinterpretation.

Hierarchy and power dynamics must also be addressed when fostering inclusivity. In some organizational cultures, junior team members may hesitate to share opinions in the presence of senior leaders. Creating an environment where all voices are encouraged requires deliberate effort. Techniques such as anonymous feedback channels, rotating facilitation roles during meetings, or explicitly inviting input from quieter participants can help level the playing field. Leaders should also model inclusive behaviors by acknowledging contributions from all team members, regardless of rank.

Inclusivity extends beyond spoken communication to the mediums and methods used. Some stakeholders may prefer formal meetings, while others thrive in less structured formats like brainstorming sessions. Adapting communication methods to suit different preferences ensures broader engagement. For example, visual learners might benefit from infographics or slide decks, while analytical thinkers may appreciate detailed reports or data-driven presentations. Providing a mix of formats caters to diverse needs and reinforces key messages across the stakeholder group.

Inclusivity requires an ongoing commitment to feedback and adaptation. Regularly soliciting input from stakeholders about the effectiveness of communication practices can highlight areas for improvement. This might involve periodic surveys, one-on-one check-ins, or debrief sessions after significant milestones. Feedback loops not only enhance communication but also demonstrate a willingness to evolve and respond to stakeholders' needs. This responsiveness fosters trust and strengthens the collaborative dynamic.

Adapting communication styles for inclusivity ensures that every stakeholder feels empowered to contribute, regardless of their background or position. By prioritizing cultural sensitivity, simplifying language, addressing power imbalances, diversifying communication methods, and incorporating feedback, organizations can build a foundation of mutual respect and understanding. Inclusive communication is not just an ethical imperative; it is a practical strategy for overcoming barriers and unlocking the full potential of diverse teams.

SUSTAINING ALIGNMENT THROUGH CONTINUOUS ENGAGEMENT

Achieving alignment among diverse stakeholders is only the beginning; sustaining that alignment requires ongoing effort and engagement. In multinational and cross-functional settings, where differences in culture, priorities, and workflows can easily cause divergence, continuous engagement is the key to maintaining collaboration, transparency, and momentum. By fostering a culture of connection and regular interaction, organizations can ensure that stakeholders remain aligned with the shared vision and procedural goals.

One of the most effective strategies for sustaining engagement is establishing regular communication touchpoints. These can take the form of weekly check-ins, monthly status updates, or quarterly strategy reviews, depending on the complexity of the initiative. Consistency is crucial—scheduled meetings or updates create a rhythm that reinforces alignment and provides opportunities for stakeholders to discuss progress, share insights, and address challenges. Using these touchpoints to reiterate the shared vision and celebrate milestones helps keep everyone focused on collective goals.

Feedback loops are another essential component of continuous engagement. Encouraging stakeholders to voice their concerns, suggestions, and observations fosters a sense of ownership and ensures that potential misalignments are identified early. Surveys, one-on-one discussions, and open forums can serve as effective channels for gathering feedback. Leaders must actively respond to this input, demonstrating that it is valued and acted upon, which in turn strengthens trust and participation among stakeholders.

Flexibility in communication methods also plays a role in maintaining alignment. Diverse stakeholders often have varying preferences and constraints, so offering multiple channels for engagement ensures inclusivity. For instance, remote teams may benefit from asynchronous tools like shared dashboards or project management software, while in-person teams might prefer face-to-face workshops. Adapting to stakeholders' changing needs—whether due to time zone differences, workload fluctuations, or technological challenges—reinforces their commitment to the process.

Recognition and appreciation are vital for sustaining motivation and engagement. Acknowledging individual and team contributions fosters a sense of achievement and reinforces alignment with the shared vision. This recognition doesn't have to be grand; even small gestures, such as a shout-out in a meeting or a personalized thank-you email, can have a significant impact. Celebrating collective successes, such as the completion of a project phase or a procedural milestone, further strengthens the sense of community and shared purpose.

Maintaining alignment requires a long-term perspective. Stakeholders must see procedural initiatives not as one-off tasks but as dynamic processes that evolve with the organization's needs. Leaders should emphasize the importance of adaptability, ensuring that procedures remain relevant and effective over time. Periodic reviews and updates, informed by stakeholder input and performance metrics, keep procedures aligned with both the organization's goals and the external environment. This iterative approach ensures that alignment is not just sustained but continuously refined.

Sustaining alignment through continuous engagement is about more than maintaining communication; it is about building relationships, fostering trust, and creating a collaborative culture. By establishing regular touchpoints, soliciting and acting on feedback, adapting to stakeholder needs, recognizing contributions, and embracing long-term adaptability, organizations can ensure that alignment remains strong even in the face of evolving challenges. Continuous engagement transforms alignment from a static achievement into an ongoing journey of collaboration and shared success.

Communication is the lifeblood of any initiative that involves diverse stakeholders. It serves as the bridge between vision and execution, between strategy and day-to-day operations. In multinational and cross-functional settings, the power of communication becomes even more critical, as it not only facilitates information sharing but also fosters trust, drives collaboration, and unites disparate groups under a shared purpose. Effective communication is not a supplementary tool; it is the cornerstone of procedural success.

At its heart, communication ensures clarity. When stakeholders from different cultural or professional backgrounds come together, misunderstandings can easily arise due to varying interpretations of goals, processes, or priorities. Clear and precise communication eliminates ambiguity, ensuring that everyone understands their roles, responsibilities, and contributions to the broader vision. Whether through detailed documentation, visual aids, or concise verbal explanations, clarity sets the stage for effective collaboration.

Communication also plays a pivotal role in building trust—a prerequisite for alignment in any diverse group. Transparent and honest exchanges create a culture of openness where stakeholders feel valued and respected. When leaders openly share updates, challenges, and successes, they signal a commitment to inclusivity and accountability. This trust encourages stakeholders to contribute their perspectives and engage wholeheartedly, knowing that their input will be acknowledged and respected.

Equally important is the ability of communication to bridge gaps in understanding. In cross-functional teams, technical jargon or field-specific language can alienate stakeholders who are unfamiliar with certain terminologies. Similarly, cultural nuances in multinational settings may lead to inadvertent misunderstandings. By prioritizing accessible language and fostering active listening, communicators can create a common ground where everyone feels comfortable participating. This inclusivity amplifies the collective intelligence of the group and drives innovation.

The emotional power of communication should not be overlooked. Words can inspire, motivate, and unite people around a common cause. Stories, metaphors, and vivid imagery have the ability to transcend logical reasoning and resonate on a deeper level, making abstract goals feel personal and achievable. For instance, sharing a narrative about how a new procedure improved outcomes in a similar organization can ignite excitement and commitment among stakeholders. Emotional resonance transforms communication from a transactional process into a transformative experience.

Communication is a dynamic force that sustains alignment over time. It is not a one-time event but an ongoing process that adapts to the evolving needs of stakeholders and the organization. Regular updates, interactive discussions, and iterative feedback loops ensure that the dialogue remains vibrant and relevant. This continuous flow of information reinforces alignment and strengthens the collaborative spirit needed to navigate challenges and seize opportunities.

The power of communication lies in its ability to transcend barriers, connect individuals, and galvanize collective action. By ensuring clarity, fostering trust, bridging understanding, evoking emotion, and sustaining alignment, communication becomes the driving force behind procedural success. In any initiative, it is the invisible thread that binds diverse stakeholders together, transforming potential discord into a harmonious and productive endeavor.

How Freelancers and Small Teams Can Implement 'Big Company' Standards on a Manageable Scale

For many freelancers and small teams, the appeal of their work lies in its freedom, flexibility, and the ability to operate without the constraints often associated with large organizations. Yet, as rewarding as this independence can be, it also brings unique challenges: inconsistent workflows, missed opportunities for efficiency, and difficulty managing growth. These obstacles often arise from a lack of structured procedures—a hallmark of "big company" operations that may seem irrelevant or inaccessible to smaller setups. However, implementing scaled-down versions of these standards can be transformative.

Standards, at their core, are not about stifling creativity or imposing bureaucracy. They are tools that bring clarity, consistency, and predictability to how work gets done. For small teams and freelancers, adopting procedures that outline how tasks are managed, decisions are made, and outcomes are measured can reduce stress, enhance professionalism, and pave the way for sustainable growth. Whether it's a simple checklist for project onboarding or a basic framework for quality assurance, these systems create a foundation for excellence without requiring the resources of a corporate giant.

The benefits of standards are particularly evident when small operations face growth or increased complexity. A freelancer expanding their client base or a small team taking on more ambitious projects will quickly realize that relying on ad-hoc methods becomes inefficient and unsustainable. Structured procedures enable scalability by providing a repeatable framework that ensures consistency in service delivery and internal workflows. They also free up cognitive energy, allowing individuals to focus on creative and strategic aspects rather than reinventing processes for every task.

Moreover, standards bring a level of professionalism that can set small operations apart in competitive markets. Clients and collaborators often associate organized procedures with reliability and expertise. A freelancer who presents a clear project timeline or a small team that adheres to defined communication protocols is more likely to earn trust and repeat business. In a world where perception matters as much as performance, structured approaches can be a differentiating factor.

This chapter will explore why standards are not just the domain of large corporations but an invaluable asset for smaller setups. It will challenge the perception that procedures are cumbersome by showing how they can be simplified, customized, and scaled to fit individual needs. By the end, readers will see that adopting standards isn't about sacrificing agility or creativity—it's about empowering themselves with the tools to thrive in any environment.

DISTILLING THE ESSENCE OF "BIG COMPANY" STANDARDS

When people think of "big company" standards, they often envision complex, rigid systems designed for sprawling corporations with thousands of employees. These might include detailed operational frameworks, exhaustive compliance protocols, or resource-intensive project management methodologies. For freelancers and small teams, such systems can seem irrelevant, intimidating, or outright incompatible with their scale and resources. However, at their foundation, these standards represent something much simpler: the pursuit of efficiency, consistency, and quality. Stripped of their corporate trappings, these principles are not just relevant to small operations—they can be transformative.

The essence of "big company" standards lies in their ability to streamline processes and minimize waste. Whether it's Lean methodologies aimed at reducing inefficiency or Six Sigma's focus on eliminating errors, these frameworks share a common goal: to make work processes as effective and predictable as possible. For small teams and freelancers, the challenge is not to replicate these systems wholesale but to adopt the principles behind them in a way that aligns with their unique workflows. This might mean replacing elaborate workflows with simple checklists or using free project management tools instead of enterprise-level software.

Another key element of corporate standards is their focus on documentation and transparency. In large organizations, clearly documented processes are essential for coordinating work across departments and ensuring consistency regardless of who is performing a task. For a freelancer or a small team, documentation serves a similar purpose. Writing down how tasks are completed, what tools are used, and what outcomes are expected creates a reference point that saves time and prevents confusion. It also allows for easy onboarding of new clients, collaborators, or team members, ensuring a seamless transition as the operation grows.

Accountability is another cornerstone of big-company practices. Large organizations rely on defined roles and responsibilities to ensure that every aspect of a project is addressed and nothing falls through the cracks. Small teams can adopt this principle by clearly assigning tasks, setting deadlines, and creating feedback loops, even if it's just among two or three people. For freelancers, personal accountability can be enhanced by implementing self-imposed deadlines and progress tracking systems. These practices foster reliability and demonstrate professionalism to clients and collaborators.

Adaptability is a lesser-known but crucial aspect of effective corporate standards. Contrary to the stereotype of rigid bureaucracy, many of the most successful companies continuously refine their procedures to respond to changing market conditions or internal needs. For small teams and freelancers, this principle is especially important. Standards should never become a source of rigidity; instead, they should serve as living tools that evolve alongside the operation. Regularly reviewing and updating procedures ensures they remain relevant and effective, allowing for growth without sacrificing agility.

By distilling the essence of big-company standards, freelancers and small teams can uncover valuable lessons without feeling overwhelmed by complexity. The focus should not be on mimicking large organizations but on adopting the principles that make them successful—efficiency, documentation, accountability, and adaptability. When approached with creativity and customization, these elements can empower even the smallest operations to achieve consistency, professionalism, and long-term success.

PRACTICAL STEPS TO IMPLEMENT SCALED-DOWN STANDARDS

For freelancers and small teams, the challenge of adopting "big company" standards lies in making them manageable and relevant. Unlike large organizations with dedicated departments to develop and enforce procedures, smaller setups must find ways to implement these practices efficiently without overloading their capacity. Fortunately, by taking deliberate, step-by-step actions, it's possible to integrate scalable and effective standards into any operation.

The first step is to identify key pain points or areas of inefficiency. Start by analyzing your current workflow. Are deadlines frequently missed? Are tasks often repeated or performed inconsistently? Does communication with clients or team members feel disorganized? By pinpointing specific problems, you can determine which areas would benefit most from structured processes. This focused approach ensures that any standards you implement address real needs, rather than adding unnecessary complexity. For example, a freelancer struggling to manage multiple clients might prioritize creating a standardized project timeline template, while a small team experiencing communication gaps might focus on setting up a shared task tracker.

Once you've identified priority areas, start small and focus on one process at a time. Trying to overhaul your entire operation at once can be overwhelming and counterproductive. Instead, choose a single workflow— such as onboarding a new client or managing a recurring task—and document the steps involved. For example, a client onboarding process might include steps like setting expectations, agreeing on deliverables, and establishing a communication schedule. Write these steps down in simple, actionable language, and test them in practice. This iterative approach allows you to refine each procedure before expanding to other areas.

Next, choose tools and technologies that align with your scale and budget. Large organizations often invest in enterprise software to manage their processes, but small setups can achieve similar results using affordable or even free tools. For instance, project management platforms like Trello or Asana are excellent for task tracking, while tools like Google Workspace or Microsoft OneDrive facilitate collaboration and documentation. The key is to choose tools that are intuitive, easy to implement, and suited to your needs. Avoid overcomplicating things; a freelancer might only need a simple spreadsheet to track tasks, while a small team might benefit from visual workflows provided by Kanban boards.

Another critical step is to involve all stakeholders in the development and implementation of these standards. Even in a small team, ensuring everyone's input and buy-in is essential for success. Collaboration fosters a sense of ownership and ensures that the procedures reflect the practical realities of the work. For freelancers working alone, this might involve gathering feedback from clients about how the process feels from their perspective. For teams, regular meetings to review and adapt new workflows can keep everyone aligned and invested.

Build a habit of monitoring and revising your standards. Procedures should never be static; they need to evolve with your business needs and external conditions. Schedule regular reviews of your workflows to assess their effectiveness and identify opportunities for improvement. For instance, if a freelancer finds that a communication template is too rigid, they can adapt it to allow for more customization. Similarly, a small team might decide to simplify task tracking if the current system becomes too cumbersome. The willingness to iterate ensures that your standards remain practical and relevant.

By following these steps—identifying pain points, starting small, leveraging the right tools, involving stakeholders, and continuously refining processes—freelancers and small teams can implement big-company standards on a scale that works for them. The result is a streamlined, professional operation capable of meeting today's challenges while preparing for tomorrow's opportunities.

LEVERAGING TECHNOLOGY FOR EFFICIENCY

Technology has revolutionized how businesses operate, offering tools that can enhance efficiency, streamline processes, and improve collaboration. While large organizations often have access to expensive enterprise solutions, freelancers and small teams can take advantage of accessible, cost-effective technologies to implement "big company" standards on a manageable scale. The key lies in selecting and utilizing tools that align with specific needs, ensuring that technology serves as an enabler rather than a burden.

The first step in leveraging technology is to identify the core processes that can benefit most from automation or digital support. For instance, freelancers might need tools to handle repetitive administrative tasks like invoicing, scheduling, or email follow-ups. Similarly, small teams managing collaborative projects can benefit from platforms that centralize communication and task tracking. By pinpointing the tasks that consume the most time or are prone to error, it becomes easier to focus on the technologies that will deliver the greatest return on investment.

Once the needs are clear, choosing the right tools becomes essential. Many technologies are designed with scalability in mind, offering functionalities tailored to small businesses and freelancers. Project management tools like Trello or ClickUp provide intuitive visual interfaces for organizing tasks and deadlines, while time-tracking apps such as Toggl can help monitor productivity. Freelancers managing multiple clients might benefit from customer relationship management (CRM) tools like HubSpot or Zoho, which simplify client tracking and communication. The key is to select tools that are not only affordable but also easy to learn and integrate into existing workflows.

Another way technology enhances efficiency is through streamlined communication and collaboration. Small teams can use platforms like Slack, Microsoft Teams, or Discord to keep communication organized and accessible, avoiding the chaos of scattered emails and messages. For file sharing and collaborative editing, cloud-based services like Google Workspace or Dropbox ensure that team members and clients have access to up-to-date information in real time. These tools also provide version control, reducing confusion and mistakes in collaborative projects. Even freelancers can use these platforms to present a more professional image to clients by sharing clear, organized deliverables.

Automation plays a particularly transformative role in implementing standards efficiently. Automation tools such as Zapier or IFTTT (If This, Then That) allow freelancers and small teams to connect different apps and create workflows that operate automatically. For example, a freelancer could use Zapier to automatically send a thank-you email after a client completes a payment or to sync task updates across platforms like Trello and Google Calendar. Small teams can set up automated reminders for deadlines or recurring meetings, reducing the cognitive load on team members and ensuring that nothing falls through the cracks.

Leveraging technology requires ongoing evaluation and adaptation. As needs evolve, the tools that were once perfect may need to be upgraded or replaced. Regularly reviewing the effectiveness of technologies ensures that they remain aligned with your goals. Are they saving time and reducing errors, or have they become cumbersome and counterproductive? Many platforms offer analytics and reporting features that provide insights into usage patterns, helping users identify what's working and what needs adjustment.

By thoughtfully integrating technology into their workflows, freelancers and small teams can achieve efficiencies that rival those of much larger organizations. The right tools not only simplify operations but also provide the structure needed to grow without losing flexibility or control. In this way, technology becomes a vital ally in applying "big company" standards at a scale that works for smaller operations.

CASE STUDIES OR ILLUSTRATIVE SCENARIOS

Real-world examples are invaluable in understanding how freelancers and small teams can successfully adopt scaled-down versions of "big company" standards. Through case studies and illustrative scenarios, we can explore practical applications of these principles and their transformative impact on small operations. These examples showcase how procedures, tools, and strategies are tailored to address specific challenges while maintaining the agility and creativity essential to smaller setups.

Case Study 1: A Freelance Graphic Designer Streamlining Client Onboarding

Sophia, a freelance graphic designer, was struggling to manage multiple clients simultaneously. Each project began differently, leading to inconsistent expectations, delays, and miscommunication. Realizing she needed structure, Sophia adopted a standardized client onboarding process inspired by corporate practices. She created a simple welcome packet outlining her services, timelines, and project phases. Using a tool like Dubsado, she automated sending contracts, collecting client information, and scheduling kickoff meetings.

This system drastically reduced her workload, allowing her to focus on creative work instead of administrative tasks. Clients appreciated the professionalism, and her streamlined process earned her referrals. Sophia's experience illustrates how a freelancer can borrow structured procedures from larger organizations to enhance efficiency and client satisfaction without sacrificing independence.

Case Study 2: A Small Marketing Team Adopting Agile Principles

A five-person marketing team at a growing startup faced challenges coordinating campaigns across social media, email, and events. Deadlines were often missed, and tasks overlapped due to unclear roles. Inspired by Agile methodologies used in larger companies, the team implemented a lightweight version of Scrum. They adopted weekly planning meetings, daily check-ins, and a shared Kanban board using Trello to track tasks.

By defining clear responsibilities and visualizing workflows, the team improved coordination and reduced duplication of efforts. Campaigns were completed on time, and team members reported feeling less stressed. This example demonstrates how small teams can adapt "big company" standards like Agile to suit their unique scale, improving both efficiency and morale.

Scenario 1: A Freelancer Applying Quality Control Procedures
Raj, a freelance software developer, often encountered post-delivery bugs in his projects, leading to dissatisfied clients and time-consuming revisions. To address this, he implemented a basic quality control procedure inspired by corporate software development practices. Raj created a checklist for testing his code before delivery, covering functionality, compatibility, and error handling. He also set up automated testing tools like Selenium for repetitive checks.

By incorporating this simple yet effective procedure, Raj drastically reduced errors, leading to happier clients and more time to take on new projects. This scenario highlights how even basic quality standards can have a significant impact when tailored to a freelancer's workflow.

Scenario 2: A Boutique Design Firm Creating a Knowledge Repository

A boutique interior design firm with three employees struggled to maintain consistency in proposals and project execution. Each team member had their own way of documenting client preferences, budgets, and design plans, leading to inefficiencies and inconsistencies. Borrowing from corporate knowledge management practices, the firm created a shared digital repository using Notion.

The repository included standardized templates for client briefs, project timelines, and vendor lists. This centralized resource ensured everyone was on the same page and saved hours of redundant work. As the firm grew, the repository became a scalable tool that maintained consistency and professionalism.

Scenario 3: Overcoming Resistance to Standards in a Small Team

A small app development team resisted adopting standardized workflows, fearing it would stifle creativity. However, as project delays and miscommunication mounted, they decided to experiment with a basic structure. The team introduced bi-weekly check-ins to set priorities and a shared Google Drive for documentation. They kept the process flexible, allowing room for brainstorming and improvisation.

Within months, the team noticed improved project timelines and clearer communication with clients. The success of this light-touch approach changed their perception of standards, showing that structure and creativity could coexist.

These case studies and scenarios illustrate how freelancers and small teams can effectively implement "big company" standards by adapting them to their specific contexts. Whether through streamlined onboarding, Agile workflows, quality control, knowledge management, or flexible team structures, these examples highlight the versatility and value of scaled-down standards.

MAINTAINING AGILITY WHILE SCALING STANDARDS

For freelancers and small teams, implementing "big company" standards often raises a concern: how to maintain the agility and adaptability that define smaller operations. Flexibility is often the competitive edge of these setups, allowing them to respond quickly to changes or new opportunities. Scaling standards effectively requires a balance between structure and the ability to pivot without being bogged down by rigid processes.

The key to maintaining agility is prioritizing simplicity over complexity when designing standards. For instance, rather than creating extensive procedure manuals, small teams can develop concise guidelines that are easy to understand and follow. A freelancer managing client projects could opt for a one-page checklist to track deliverables, deadlines, and communications instead of an elaborate project management framework. This approach ensures that procedures enhance efficiency without becoming cumbersome or time-consuming.

Another critical strategy is to embed flexibility into the standards themselves. Procedures should serve as frameworks rather than strict rules, allowing room for adjustments based on the situation. For example, a small graphic design team could standardize their creative process by defining broad stages—such as research, conceptualization, and delivery—while leaving space for individual designers to adapt their approach within those stages. This ensures consistency while preserving creative freedom and responsiveness to client needs.

Technology can also play a pivotal role in balancing structure and agility. Using dynamic tools that facilitate customization enables smaller operations to scale standards without sacrificing adaptability. For instance, project management platforms like Asana or Monday.com allow users to create flexible workflows that can be easily modified as projects evolve. Similarly, tools like Airtable combine the structure of databases with the flexibility of spreadsheets, offering a scalable way to manage tasks and data while accommodating individual preferences.

Regular feedback and iteration are essential for keeping standards agile. By fostering a culture of continuous improvement, teams can ensure that their processes remain relevant and effective over time. Freelancers can gather feedback from clients to refine their workflows, while small teams can conduct periodic reviews to assess which procedures are working and which need adjustments. For example, a small marketing team might realize that their task-tracking system is too detailed for fast-paced campaigns and simplify it accordingly. This iterative approach prevents standards from becoming outdated or overly restrictive.

Maintaining agility while scaling standards requires a mindset shift: viewing procedures as enablers of adaptability rather than constraints. Well-designed standards free up mental bandwidth by reducing inefficiencies and ambiguities, enabling individuals and teams to focus on higher-level decision-making. For instance, a standardized template for client proposals saves time and ensures professionalism, allowing team members to dedicate more energy to creative solutions or strategic planning.

By embracing simplicity, embedding flexibility, leveraging technology, iterating processes, and shifting perceptions, freelancers and small teams can scale standards in ways that enhance rather than hinder agility. This balance allows them to enjoy the best of both worlds—structured efficiency and the freedom to innovate and adapt as needed.

ACTIONABLE TAKEAWAYS FOR FREELANCERS AND SMALL TEAMS

Freelancers and small teams face unique challenges when it comes to adopting and maintaining scalable standards, but with the right mindset and tools, they can turn these challenges into opportunities for growth. Below are practical, actionable strategies to help implement "big company" standards on a manageable scale while staying efficient and adaptable.

1. Start Small and Build Gradually

Avoid overhauling your entire workflow overnight. Instead, identify one or two areas where introducing standards could make an immediate impact. For freelancers, this might be standardizing client onboarding with templates for proposals and contracts. Small teams might start by implementing a shared calendar or task management tool. Building gradually allows you to refine processes without feeling overwhelmed.

2. Use Templates and Checklists

Templates and checklists provide structure while remaining easy to adapt. Freelancers can create reusable templates for contracts, project briefs, or invoices to ensure consistency and save time. Similarly, small teams can standardize processes with checklists for recurring tasks like marketing campaigns or product launches. These tools act as simple yet powerful anchors for maintaining quality and professionalism.

3. Embrace Technology as an Enabler

Leverage accessible and affordable technology to simplify workflows and implement standards. Tools like Trello, Asana, or Notion can help manage projects and tasks collaboratively, while apps like QuickBooks or FreshBooks streamline financial tracking for freelancers. Choose tools that align with your needs and are intuitive to use, ensuring that they enhance efficiency rather than add complexity.

4. Prioritize Communication

Standards are only effective if everyone involved understands and embraces them. Clearly communicate the purpose and benefits of new procedures to your team or clients, and encourage feedback. Use tools like Slack or

Microsoft Teams to keep communication streamlined and organized, reducing the risk of misalignment. For freelancers, regular client check-ins can clarify expectations and foster trust.

5. Make Standards Flexible and Scalable

Avoid rigid processes that can't adapt to changing circumstances. Design standards as frameworks rather than strict rules, leaving room for creativity and customization. For example, a small software development team might standardize coding practices but allow developers to choose their preferred tools for testing or debugging. Flexibility ensures that standards remain relevant as needs evolve.

6. Measure and Refine Your Processes

Track the effectiveness of your standards by measuring outcomes like time saved, client satisfaction, or error reduction. Use these insights to tweak and improve your workflows. For example, a small team using a project management tool can analyze task completion rates to identify bottlenecks, while a freelancer might refine their proposal template based on client feedback.

7. Invest in Learning and Growth

Develop your understanding of industry best practices and tools. Online courses, webinars, and communities can provide insights into how other small operations implement standards. This not only keeps you updated on trends but also sparks ideas for improving your own processes. Freelancers might explore productivity apps, while small teams can learn about lightweight versions of Agile or Lean methodologies.

8. Focus on Consistency Over Perfection

Standards don't need to be flawless to be effective. Aim for consistency in how tasks are approached and executed, even if the processes evolve over time. This consistency builds trust with clients, team members, and other stakeholders, laying the foundation for long-term success.

9. Align Standards with Your Goals

Ensure that every standard you implement supports your broader objectives. For freelancers, this might mean creating workflows that allow for faster turnaround times, improving client satisfaction. Small teams might prioritize standards that enhance collaboration or reduce errors, enabling them to scale their operations efficiently.

10. Celebrate Small Wins

Recognize and celebrate the improvements brought about by your efforts. For example, if a new checklist reduces client revision requests or a project management tool shortens delivery times, acknowledge these successes. Celebrating small wins boosts morale and reinforces the value of maintaining standards.

By applying these takeaways, freelancers and small teams can not only implement "big company" standards effectively but also enhance their productivity, professionalism, and ability to scale. These steps empower smaller operations to compete in larger markets without losing the creativity and agility that set them apart.

Continuous Improvement and Innovation

The interplay between procedures and creativity is often viewed as a conflict, with structured processes dismissed as stifling the free flow of ideas. This perception, while common, overlooks the nuanced relationship where each can complement and enhance the other. Procedures are often seen as rigid frameworks designed to enforce compliance and uniformity. On the other hand, creativity thrives on freedom and unpredictability, drawing strength from the absence of constraints. Yet, history and practice reveal a different story—one where procedures can serve as a springboard for innovation rather than a barrier.

Consider the realm of industrial design or software development, where adherence to processes like Lean or Agile methodologies has led to groundbreaking advancements. These approaches were initially implemented to optimize efficiency, yet they have also fostered environments where creativity can flourish. By setting clear boundaries, these frameworks provide the structure necessary for teams to experiment, iterate, and ultimately innovate. This paradoxical relationship shows that procedures, when applied thoughtfully, do not suppress creativity but rather channel it into productive outcomes.

The rise of creative constraints as a concept further supports this perspective. Studies in psychology and innovation reveal that creativity often flourishes within limitations. Boundaries, rather than restricting ideation, can focus efforts and direct energy toward finding unique solutions. In a workplace setting, this could mean the difference between aimless brainstorming and targeted, impactful innovation. Without structure, creative efforts risk devolving into chaos, whereas well-designed processes provide the scaffolding needed to bring imaginative ideas to fruition.

Real-world examples underline the viability of this balance. Pixar, for instance, has famously maintained a structured process for storytelling that incorporates iterative feedback and collaborative revisions. Their adherence to these procedures has not hindered their ability to produce some of the most original and creative films in modern history. Similarly, IT companies employing Agile workflows regularly demonstrate how structured sprints and clear objectives can coexist with, and even amplify, innovative solutions to complex problems.

This chapter delves into the symbiotic relationship between procedures and creativity, challenging the assumption that one must come at the expense of the other. Through theoretical insights, practical strategies, and compelling case studies, it will uncover how organizations and individuals can strike this balance. Far from being oppositional forces, procedures and creativity, when harmonized, become powerful drivers of progress and innovation.

THEORETICAL UNDERPINNINGS

At first glance, procedures and creativity seem to operate on opposite ends of a spectrum: one emphasizes order and predictability, while the other thrives on freedom and spontaneity. However, psychological and organizational theories suggest that these two forces are not only compatible but can be mutually reinforcing. The concept of "creative constraints" emerges as a key idea in this interplay, underscoring how boundaries and frameworks can enhance, rather than diminish, creative output.

Creative constraints are rooted in cognitive psychology, where research shows that limitations can sharpen focus and inspire innovation. When individuals or teams work within defined parameters, their problem-solving abilities are often heightened as they seek unconventional solutions to overcome barriers. This is evident in areas like design and engineering, where constraints such as limited budgets, tight deadlines, or specific client requirements often lead to ingenious breakthroughs. These constraints act as a catalyst, compelling individuals to think more deeply and strategically.

Organizational behavior studies further reinforce the value of structure in fostering creativity. Theories such as Amabile's Componential Theory of Creativity highlight the role of intrinsic motivation, domain-relevant skills, and a conducive work environment in generating creative outcomes. Procedures, when designed thoughtfully, contribute to this environment by reducing uncertainty and providing a clear framework for exploration. For instance, methodologies like Agile and Lean are predicated on iterative cycles and regular feedback, both of which encourage experimentation within a structured process.

A critical element in this dynamic is the balance between rigidity and flexibility. Research on innovation emphasizes that overly rigid procedures can indeed stifle creativity by creating a fear of failure or discouraging exploration. However, when processes incorporate flexibility—such as allowing teams to adapt workflows or providing autonomy within set objectives—they create a "sandbox" where creativity can thrive. This concept aligns with Deci and Ryan's Self-Determination Theory, which suggests that autonomy, competence, and relatedness are essential for intrinsic motivation and creative engagement.

The intersection of creativity and procedures also extends to systems theory, where the interplay of components within a structured framework can generate emergent properties. For example, cross-functional collaboration within a well-defined process can produce insights and solutions that no individual team member could achieve alone. This systems-oriented approach illustrates how procedures can act as enablers of collective creativity, allowing diverse perspectives to converge in innovative ways.

By understanding these theoretical foundations, it becomes clear that procedures are not inherently at odds with creativity. Instead, they provide the scaffolding necessary to channel creative energy into purposeful innovation. As we examine practical strategies in the next sections, these theories will serve as a lens for evaluating how organizations and individuals can optimize the balance between structure and creativity.

SYNERGY BETWEEN STRUCTURE AND CREATIVITY

The relationship between structure and creativity is not inherently adversarial; rather, it is symbiotic when managed effectively. Structure provides the clarity and stability needed to organize efforts, while creativity injects adaptability and ingenuity into processes. Together, they form a dynamic partnership that enables individuals and organizations to solve problems, innovate, and achieve sustainable success. This synergy is especially evident in fields like IT development, industrial processes, and other domains where structured methodologies coexist with creative breakthroughs.

One of the clearest demonstrations of this synergy lies in the Agile methodology widely used in software development and project management. Agile frameworks, such as Scrum, rely on structured workflows like sprints, stand-up meetings, and defined deliverables. These processes establish clear goals and timelines, ensuring accountability and focus. At the same time, Agile emphasizes adaptability, allowing teams to pivot in response to new information or challenges. This balance between fixed frameworks and iterative creativity has been instrumental in driving innovation in fast-paced industries.

A similar pattern is observed in industrialized processes, where Lean principles are used to eliminate waste and optimize efficiency without sacrificing innovation. Companies such as Toyota have pioneered Lean systems that encourage continuous improvement through employee involvement and structured problem-solving. By empowering workers to identify inefficiencies and propose solutions, these organizations have shown that structured procedures can be a platform for bottom-up creativity. This approach not only improves operational outcomes but also fosters a culture of engagement and innovation.

From a psychological perspective, structure creates the mental space needed for creativity to flourish. Without clear processes, teams and individuals often face ambiguity, which can lead to decision fatigue and diminished focus. Procedures reduce this cognitive load by providing a roadmap for action, freeing mental bandwidth for creative ideation. For example, brainstorming sessions within a well-structured agenda often yield more actionable ideas than open-ended discussions. The structure ensures that creativity is harnessed productively rather than dissipating into uncoordinated effort.

Case studies reinforce this interplay. Take Pixar, a company renowned for its creative excellence, which operates within a highly structured storytelling process. Each film undergoes rigorous stages of development, including storyboarding, peer review, and iterative revisions. These procedures do not stifle creativity; instead, they channel it into cohesive, high-quality narratives. Similarly, in the pharmaceutical industry, companies balance rigid regulatory compliance with innovative drug discovery processes. Here, strict protocols ensure safety and efficacy while fostering breakthroughs in medical science.

The synergy between structure and creativity depends on recognizing their complementary roles. Structure does not merely impose order; it acts as a foundation on which creativity can thrive. Conversely, creativity invigorates procedures, ensuring they remain relevant and adaptable in a changing world. By integrating these forces thoughtfully, organizations and individuals can unlock their full potential, achieving results that neither could accomplish alone. This synergy is not only a best practice but a necessity for success in today's complex, innovation-driven environments.

CHALLENGES IN BALANCING BOTH

Striking the right balance between procedures and creativity is no small feat. While the two can coexist harmoniously, achieving this synergy often involves navigating a series of challenges that arise at both the organizational and individual levels. These challenges, if left unaddressed, can lead to missed opportunities for innovation, reduced efficiency, and employee disengagement. Understanding these obstacles is the first step toward effectively managing them.

One of the primary challenges is the perception of incompatibility. Many organizations view creativity and structure as opposing forces, leading to a preference for one at the expense of the other. This dichotomy often results in rigid procedures that stifle innovation or, conversely, in unstructured environments where creativity lacks direction. For example, overly prescriptive workflows in traditional industries can discourage employees from proposing novel ideas, fearing that deviations from the standard will be met with resistance or penalties. Conversely, in startups or creative agencies, the absence of clear processes can lead to inefficiency and burnout, as teams struggle to prioritize tasks or measure progress.

Another challenge lies in organizational culture. Companies with deeply entrenched hierarchical systems may struggle to foster creativity within procedural frameworks. Employees in such environments often feel disempowered to challenge established norms or experiment with new approaches. On the other hand, organizations that prioritize flexibility and innovation may undervalue the importance of procedural consistency, resulting in chaotic workflows and inconsistent outcomes. Balancing these cultural tendencies requires deliberate leadership that champions both structure and creative freedom.

At the individual level, cognitive biases can also pose significant challenges. The status quo bias, for instance, may lead employees to resist changes to established procedures, even when such changes are clearly beneficial. Conversely, the novelty bias can drive a preference for untested ideas over proven methods, causing teams to abandon effective procedures in pursuit of unfeasible innovations. Addressing these biases requires fostering a mindset that values both procedural reliability and creative exploration, emphasizing the benefits of integrating the two.

A lack of communication and alignment exacerbates these challenges. In cross-functional teams, misaligned priorities and conflicting interpretations of processes can create friction between departments. For example, a marketing team focused on creative campaigns may clash with an operations team prioritizing compliance and efficiency. Without mechanisms to bridge these gaps, such conflicts can hinder collaboration and stifle both procedural adherence and innovative outcomes.

Scalability presents a unique hurdle. What works for small teams may not translate to larger organizations. Procedures designed to foster creativity at the team level may become overly complex or bureaucratic when scaled across departments or global operations. Similarly, innovative practices that emerge organically in smaller settings often lose their effectiveness when subjected to rigid corporate structures. Scaling these approaches requires tailoring them to fit the unique needs and dynamics of larger organizations.

Balancing procedures and creativity demands a nuanced approach that recognizes and addresses these challenges. Organizations must shift from an "either-or" mindset to a "both-and" perspective, fostering cultures that value structure as a facilitator rather than an inhibitor of creativity. By tackling these obstacles proactively, leaders can create environments where creativity and procedures coexist productively, driving sustainable innovation and operational excellence.

STRATEGIES TO FOSTER CREATIVITY WITHIN PROCEDURES

Creating a productive environment where creativity thrives within the boundaries of well-defined procedures requires intentional strategies. Organizations and individuals alike must adopt methods that embrace structure as a platform for innovation rather than a constraint. These strategies range from cultural shifts to practical tools, ensuring that creativity remains integral to achieving both short-term goals and long-term vision.

The first strategy involves designing flexible frameworks that encourage experimentation. Procedures should establish clear objectives and guidelines while leaving room for variation in how those goals are achieved. For example, project management methodologies like Agile use sprints and retrospectives to ensure accountability but allow teams the freedom to adapt workflows and priorities as circumstances evolve. This approach empowers teams to innovate within a structured timeline, balancing creativity with discipline.

Another effective strategy is the incorporation of feedback loops into procedural design. Feedback loops create iterative opportunities for reflection and improvement, ensuring that processes remain adaptable and responsive. In practice, this can involve regular brainstorming sessions, post-project reviews, or digital tools that collect real-time input from employees. For instance, many organizations use customer feedback to refine products through controlled iterations, ensuring that innovation aligns with user needs while adhering to procedural standards.

Cross-functional collaboration is another essential strategy for fostering creativity within structured environments. By bringing together individuals from diverse disciplines, organizations can generate fresh ideas that challenge conventional thinking. For example, pairing a creative marketing team with a data-driven operations team can lead to innovative campaigns grounded in analytical insights. To make this collaboration effective, clear procedural guidelines—such as shared goals and communication protocols—should be in place to prevent misalignment and friction.

Providing autonomy within boundaries is equally crucial. Employees should feel empowered to make decisions and explore new ideas within the safety net of established processes. Companies like Google famously allocate "20% time," allowing employees to work on passion projects that might benefit the organization. Though this freedom exists within broader operational frameworks, it has led to groundbreaking innovations like Gmail and Google Maps. Similarly, smaller-scale initiatives, such as giving teams control over specific aspects of a project, can foster a sense of ownership and encourage creative solutions.

Leaders must also cultivate a culture of psychological safety, where employees feel confident in expressing unconventional ideas without fear of judgment or failure. This can be achieved by celebrating experimentation and reframing failures as learning opportunities. For instance, organizations like 3M actively reward employees for innovative contributions, regardless of whether every idea leads to success. Establishing this culture ensures that creativity is not stifled by fear of deviating from established norms.

Leveraging technological tools can enhance creativity within procedures. Digital platforms like collaborative software, design-thinking apps, or AI-driven analytics streamline routine tasks, freeing up time for innovative pursuits. For instance, automation in repetitive processes allows teams to focus on higher-value activities, such as ideation and strategic planning. Technology also enables real-time communication and resource-sharing, essential for fostering creativity in distributed teams.

By integrating these strategies, organizations can transform procedures into enablers of creativity rather than barriers. These methods ensure that processes remain robust yet adaptable, providing the structure needed for sustained operational excellence while inspiring innovation at every level. Such an approach not only drives better outcomes but also builds a culture of continuous improvement and creative empowerment.

The balance between structure and creativity is not a fixed endpoint but an ongoing process that evolves alongside organizational needs and individual goals. Throughout this chapter, we've explored how structure can serve as a launchpad for innovation rather than an obstacle, and how creativity breathes life into otherwise static procedures. This interplay, when managed thoughtfully, creates a dynamic environment where processes drive productivity without stifling originality.

As demonstrated through real-world examples and theoretical insights, the tension between structure and creativity is often misunderstood. Rigid systems are mistakenly seen as the antithesis of innovation, while unstructured creativity is viewed as incompatible with operational efficiency. However, the key lies in reframing these forces as complementary rather than contradictory. When paired effectively, structure provides the foundation and direction needed to transform creative ideas into actionable solutions, ensuring that innovation is both sustainable and scalable.

The challenges in achieving this balance are undeniable. From overcoming organizational inertia to fostering a culture that values experimentation, success requires intentional strategies and leadership. Addressing biases, aligning cross-functional teams, and scaling processes to match the complexity of larger operations are pivotal steps. These obstacles, though significant, present opportunities to rethink and redesign systems to accommodate both consistency and ingenuity.

Strategies such as building flexible frameworks, incorporating feedback loops, and promoting psychological safety empower individuals and teams to navigate this balance. Moreover, tools like technology and cross-functional collaboration offer practical ways to integrate creativity into daily operations, ensuring that innovation is a continuous and inclusive effort. These methods remind us that procedures are not mere checklists but powerful enablers of growth and discovery.

Ultimately, the coexistence of creativity and structure is not just a best practice but a necessity in today's fast-paced, innovation-driven world. Organizations that master this balance will not only enhance their competitiveness but also create workplaces where employees feel valued, empowered, and inspired to contribute their best ideas. For individuals, embracing this mindset can lead to greater satisfaction and fulfillment, transforming routine tasks into opportunities for ingenuity and progress.

In redefining the relationship between structure and creativity, we open the door to endless possibilities. By championing both, we equip ourselves to tackle complex challenges, seize emerging opportunities, and build a future where innovation and efficiency thrive together. The journey requires effort and adaptability, but the rewards—for individuals, organizations, and society—are immeasurable.

ACTIONABLE TIPS FOR BALANCING PROCEDURES AND CREATIVITY

Balancing procedures and creativity requires a deliberate approach that integrates structured processes with opportunities for innovation. This balance is not merely theoretical but demands practical strategies that individuals and organizations can implement. The following actionable tips provide a roadmap to cultivate environments where procedures support creative thinking, and creativity enhances the effectiveness of structured workflows.

Adopt Agile Methodologies for Flexibility Within Structure

Agile frameworks, originally developed for software development, are versatile tools that can help manage the interplay between creativity and procedures across various industries. By breaking down projects into smaller, iterative stages—known as sprints—teams can maintain focus on defined objectives while experimenting and adjusting along the way.

In practice:

- Use regular stand-up meetings to assess progress and identify roadblocks, ensuring alignment without stifling new ideas.

- Incorporate retrospectives at the end of each sprint to reflect on what worked and what didn't, fostering continuous improvement.

- Empower teams to reprioritize tasks within the sprint, allowing space for creative problem-solving.

Agile approaches provide structure while maintaining flexibility, ensuring that creativity thrives within manageable boundaries.

Foster a Culture of Psychological Safety

Creativity flourishes when individuals feel safe to voice unconventional ideas without fear of ridicule or reprimand. Psychological safety is the foundation of this openness and must be actively nurtured. Leaders play a critical role in creating an environment where experimentation and even failure are embraced as part of the learning process.

In practice:

- Celebrate creative attempts, even those that fail, as valuable contributions to innovation.

- Encourage all team members, regardless of rank or role, to share ideas during brainstorming sessions.

- Model vulnerability by sharing your own experiences with failure and learning, demonstrating that mistakes are stepping stones rather than barriers.

This culture helps employees see procedures not as rigid constraints but as scaffolding that supports their creative endeavors.

Build Flexibility Into Procedures

Rigid, overly detailed procedures can stifle creativity by leaving little room for variation. To encourage innovation, organizations should design processes that outline key steps or objectives but allow for flexibility in how they are achieved.

In practice:

- Use principles-based guidelines rather than step-by-step instructions for tasks that require creativity. For instance, instead of prescribing exact methods for product design, provide outcome-based criteria.

- Include "innovation checkpoints" in workflows, where teams pause to evaluate alternative approaches or consider creative solutions.

- Allow teams to deviate from established procedures when justified by evidence or unique circumstances, formalizing this through a review process to maintain accountability.

These adaptable structures ensure consistency while giving teams the freedom to explore novel solutions.

Incorporate Feedback Loops for Continuous Improvement

Feedback loops are essential for refining processes and fostering creativity. They provide opportunities to learn from successes and failures, enabling teams to adapt procedures to better support innovative thinking.

In practice:

- Schedule regular debriefs or after-action reviews where teams analyze what worked and identify areas for improvement.

- Use anonymous feedback tools to gather honest input from employees about how procedures might be hindering creativity.

- Implement customer feedback as part of product development, encouraging teams to iterate based on real-world insights.

Feedback loops not only improve processes but also validate the contributions of creative individuals, reinforcing their commitment to innovation.

Leverage Technology to Streamline Repetitive Tasks

Automation and digital tools can free up time and resources, allowing teams to focus on higher-order creative work. By reducing the cognitive load associated with routine procedures, technology creates bandwidth for brainstorming and experimentation.

In practice:

- Use project management software to handle task tracking, timelines, and resource allocation. Tools like Trello or Asana streamline coordination, leaving more space for ideation.
- Automate data collection and analysis with tools like Tableau or Power BI, enabling teams to focus on interpreting insights rather than gathering them.
- Employ AI tools for idea generation or rapid prototyping, providing a starting point for creative discussions.

When technology handles the mundane, creativity can take center stage.

Encourage Cross-Functional Collaboration

Innovation often arises from the intersection of diverse perspectives. By facilitating collaboration across departments or disciplines, organizations can harness a broader range of ideas and insights.

In practice:

- Create mixed teams for major projects, pairing analytical thinkers with creative problem-solvers.
- Host regular "innovation labs" where employees from different departments tackle hypothetical or real-world challenges together.
- Encourage job shadowing or rotational roles to help employees understand how their work connects to other functions, sparking new ideas for collaboration.

Cross-functional collaboration prevents siloed thinking and ensures that creativity informs procedural design.

Provide Structured Opportunities for Experimentation

Innovation requires deliberate investment in time and resources for experimentation. Organizations should formalize this by setting aside dedicated periods or projects specifically for creative exploration.

In practice:

- Establish "innovation days" where teams step away from regular duties to focus on generating and testing new ideas.
- Create innovation funds that employees can access to pilot creative projects with minimal risk.
- Encourage small-scale experimentation by allowing teams to test new ideas within limited scopes before scaling them across the organization.

These opportunities signal that creativity is not only welcomed but integral to success.

Measure and Reward Creativity

While processes are often evaluated through metrics like efficiency or compliance, creativity must also be measured and celebrated. Doing so reinforces its value and encourages employees to integrate innovative thinking into their workflows.

In practice:

- Develop key performance indicators (KPIs) for innovation, such as the number of ideas implemented or the impact of creative projects on business outcomes.
- Recognize and reward teams or individuals who propose innovative solutions, even if those ideas don't always result in immediate success.
- Share success stories of procedural creativity in company communications, inspiring others to follow suit.

Acknowledging creative contributions alongside procedural achievements fosters a holistic approach to performance.

Train Leaders to Balance Creativity and Structure

Leadership plays a pivotal role in maintaining the balance between procedures and innovation. Leaders must develop the skills to guide teams through structured workflows while encouraging creative contributions.

In practice:

- Provide training on innovation management, teaching leaders how to integrate creativity into procedural frameworks.

- Encourage leaders to act as facilitators, asking open-ended questions and challenging assumptions rather than imposing rigid solutions.

- Use leadership development programs to promote emotional intelligence and adaptability, essential traits for fostering creativity.

Well-trained leaders set the tone for an organization that values both structure and innovation.

By implementing these actionable strategies, organizations can create a culture where procedures serve as a foundation for creative exploration rather than a barrier to it. Balancing structure and creativity requires effort, but the rewards—greater innovation, improved efficiency, and enhanced employee engagement—make it an essential endeavor for any forward-thinking organization.

The role of feedback loops in refining processes

In the world of processes and systems, feedback loops are the invisible architects shaping continuous improvement and innovation. Their essence lies in the iterative exchange of information, where outputs of a system inform its future actions. This concept, borrowed from systems theory, transcends academic abstraction and finds practical utility in the workplace, whether in IT, manufacturing, healthcare, or creative industries. Feedback loops are not static elements of a system; they are dynamic, enabling organizations to adapt and refine their practices in response to both internal and external stimuli.

The term "feedback loop" originates from engineering and biology, where it describes a system's ability to self-regulate through the cyclical exchange of information. In business contexts, it has evolved to signify the structured processes through which organizations collect data, analyze it, and apply insights to refine operations. This evolution reflects a broader shift in organizational thinking—from rigid, hierarchical control to adaptive, iterative methodologies. In this way, feedback loops have become indispensable to maintaining relevance in environments defined by constant change and competition.

One of the most compelling aspects of feedback loops is their duality. Positive feedback loops amplify changes, often driving growth or innovation by reinforcing successful outcomes. Conversely, negative feedback loops stabilize systems, correcting deviations and ensuring that operations align with established standards or goals. Both types are essential in the workplace, creating a balance between fostering innovation and maintaining order. For example, an IT team may use a positive loop to accelerate software updates based on user demand, while simultaneously employing a negative loop to resolve bugs and maintain system reliability.

Feedback loops also play a critical role in aligning organizational goals with daily execution. Consider a multinational company managing supply chains across continents. Without a mechanism to gather and act on real-time data—feedback from shipping delays, supplier issues, or fluctuating demand—the company risks inefficiency and financial loss. Feedback loops bridge this gap, ensuring that strategic decisions are informed by the realities on the ground. By integrating these mechanisms into every level of operation, organizations can achieve a level of responsiveness that sets them apart in their industries.

However, the value of feedback loops is not merely operational; it is cultural. They create an environment where employees at all levels feel heard, valued, and empowered to contribute to the organization's success. When properly implemented, feedback mechanisms democratize decision-making, breaking down silos and encouraging collaboration. This fosters a sense of ownership and accountability, transforming feedback from a tool for management into a shared resource for organizational growth. As such, feedback loops are more than systems of refinement—they are catalysts for innovation, inclusion, and sustained success.

THE IMPORTANCE OF FEEDBACK LOOPS IN PROCESS REFINEMENT

Feedback loops are the lifeblood of process refinement, transforming static systems into dynamic ones capable of evolving with changing circumstances. At their nucleus, feedback loops serve as mechanisms of evaluation and improvement, ensuring that processes do not stagnate or fall prey to inefficiencies. They provide a structured way to collect information, analyze outcomes, and implement changes that align operations more closely with organizational goals. In an age where adaptability is key, feedback loops are the foundation upon which successful and sustainable processes are built.

The primary value of feedback loops lies in their ability to detect and correct inefficiencies. Processes, no matter how meticulously designed, often face unforeseen challenges or become outdated over time. A supply chain procedure might initially operate efficiently but encounter delays due to shifts in supplier capabilities or geopolitical disruptions. Feedback loops identify these gaps, enabling organizations to course-correct in real time. Without this cyclical mechanism of refinement, processes risk becoming rigid relics, unable to adapt to an ever-changing business environment.

Moreover, feedback loops foster alignment between strategic objectives and operational realities. For instance, in IT development, agile methodologies rely heavily on iterative feedback to ensure projects meet client expectations while staying on schedule. Regular retrospectives—meetings designed to evaluate what went well, what didn't, and what could be improved—are an example of how feedback loops drive alignment. These sessions transform abstract goals, such as "enhancing user experience," into actionable insights that directly influence development priorities. In this way, feedback loops act as the connective tissue between high-level strategies and ground-level execution.

Another critical role of feedback loops is in cultivating a culture of accountability and engagement. When employees see that their insights are not only heard but acted upon, it fosters a sense of ownership and trust within the organization. For example, frontline workers in a manufacturing plant often possess unique knowledge of inefficiencies or risks that upper management may overlook. Incorporating their feedback into process improvements not only optimizes operations but also strengthens morale and reduces resistance to change. The collaborative nature of feedback loops thus enhances both the technical and human aspects of organizational processes.

Feedback loops are essential drivers of innovation. By continually evaluating outcomes and incorporating diverse perspectives, organizations create fertile ground for new ideas to emerge. A customer service team, for example, might identify recurring complaints about a product that inspire the development of an entirely new feature. This iterative process ensures that creativity is not stifled by rigid adherence to outdated procedures but is instead integrated into the refinement cycle. Through feedback loops, organizations not only improve existing processes but also discover opportunities for breakthrough advancements.

Feedback loops are indispensable for refining processes in a meaningful and sustainable way. They address inefficiencies, align strategy with execution, foster a culture of accountability, and drive innovation. By embracing feedback as a continuous and integral part of operations, organizations position themselves to thrive in complex and rapidly changing environments. The importance of feedback loops cannot be overstated—they are the engines of progress in an increasingly dynamic world.

KEY COMPONENTS OF EFFECTIVE FEEDBACK LOOPS

Effective feedback loops are not mere mechanisms of data collection; they are intricate systems requiring thoughtful design, execution, and monitoring. Their impact lies in the ability to generate actionable insights that refine processes and enhance outcomes. Understanding the key components of these loops is essential for ensuring they function as intended. These elements include clear objectives, robust data collection methods, timely communication, actionable analysis, and consistent follow-through. Together, these components create a seamless cycle of learning and improvement that drives organizational growth.

The foundation of any effective feedback loop is clarity of purpose. Without a well-defined objective, the data collected may lack relevance, leading to misaligned efforts and wasted resources. For example, in an IT project, the goal of a feedback loop might be to optimize the user interface for a specific demographic. This clarity ensures that the feedback focuses on aspects directly tied to the goal, such as usability metrics or user satisfaction surveys, rather than tangential issues. Clear objectives also provide a benchmark for evaluating the success of the loop, making it easier to measure progress over time.

Robust data collection methods form the second pillar of effective feedback loops. The quality and reliability of the data gathered directly influence the loop's ability to generate meaningful insights. This requires selecting appropriate tools and techniques for capturing feedback, whether through customer surveys, performance analytics, or team retrospectives. For example, in manufacturing, sensors on production lines can provide real-time data on equipment efficiency, while employee suggestions might highlight practical improvements overlooked by automation. Combining quantitative and qualitative data ensures a comprehensive understanding of the system's performance.

Timely communication is another critical component. Feedback must be gathered and shared within a timeframe that allows for prompt action. Delayed insights risk becoming obsolete, particularly in fast-moving industries like technology or healthcare. Real-time dashboards, weekly performance reviews, or iterative sprint meetings are examples of mechanisms that keep feedback loops dynamic and relevant. Effective communication also extends to how feedback is presented—clear, concise, and tailored to the audience. For instance, technical teams may benefit from detailed metrics, while executives might require high-level summaries with actionable takeaways.

Actionable analysis transforms raw data into meaningful insights. This step involves identifying patterns, root causes, and areas for improvement, ensuring that the feedback translates into clear next steps. Tools such as root cause analysis, predictive analytics, or machine learning can enhance the precision of this process. For example, a retail company analyzing customer complaints may discover that delays in delivery are linked to a specific distribution center. Actionable analysis ensures that feedback loops do more than highlight problems—they pave the way for targeted, effective solutions.

Consistent follow-through ensures the feedback loop's efficacy. This involves implementing the insights gained, monitoring the outcomes of changes made, and re-entering the loop for further refinement. Without this step, feedback becomes a theoretical exercise rather than a driver of real improvement. For instance, an organization addressing high employee turnover might collect feedback through exit interviews, implement changes based on common themes (e.g., workload or management style), and reassess turnover rates to gauge the effectiveness of the intervention. This iterative process ensures that improvements are sustained and continuously optimized.

Effective feedback loops rely on five interconnected components: clear objectives, robust data collection, timely communication, actionable analysis, and consistent follow-through. Each plays a distinct role in creating a feedback system that is not only efficient but also impactful. By understanding and implementing these elements, organizations can unlock the full potential of feedback loops, transforming them into powerful tools for process refinement and innovation.

REAL-WORLD APPLICATIONS OF FEEDBACK LOOPS

Feedback loops are not merely theoretical constructs; their practical applications span industries and disciplines, driving improvements in diverse contexts. From manufacturing and healthcare to IT and customer service, these loops enable organizations to adapt, optimize, and innovate. The effectiveness of feedback loops lies in their ability to translate real-time observations into actionable changes, enhancing both efficiency and outcomes. Examining their real-world applications reveals the transformative potential of feedback loops in addressing complex challenges and fostering continuous improvement.

In the manufacturing sector, feedback loops have been a cornerstone of quality control and efficiency. Techniques like Six Sigma rely heavily on feedback loops to identify defects, streamline processes, and reduce waste. Sensors embedded in production lines capture data on machinery performance, while visual inspections and employee input add qualitative insights. For example, an automotive company might use real-time monitoring to detect inconsistencies in assembly, allowing for immediate adjustments to prevent larger defects. Over time, this iterative process not only improves product quality but also reduces costs, underscoring the tangible benefits of feedback loops in operational excellence.

Healthcare provides another compelling example of feedback loops in action. Patient care often hinges on the ability to collect, analyze, and act upon feedback rapidly. In hospital settings, tools like patient satisfaction surveys, electronic health records, and wearable devices generate data that inform treatment decisions and service improvements. For instance, a hospital might use feedback from post-discharge surveys to identify gaps in communication about medication, leading to revised protocols that enhance patient outcomes. Feedback loops in healthcare also extend to medical research, where ongoing clinical trials depend on iterative feedback to refine treatments and protocols.

The IT industry exemplifies the use of feedback loops in agile development. Agile methodologies prioritize iterative progress, incorporating continuous feedback from stakeholders and end-users to refine software and address issues early in the development cycle. For example, a tech company developing a new app might release a beta version to a select group of users, gathering insights on usability and performance. These inputs inform subsequent iterations, ensuring the final product aligns with user needs. The feedback loop not only accelerates innovation but also reduces the risk of costly errors, making it a critical component of successful software development.

In customer service, feedback loops are instrumental in improving the user experience and maintaining brand loyalty. Companies often rely on tools like Net Promoter Scores (NPS), social media monitoring, and customer support analytics to gather insights into consumer satisfaction. For instance, an e-commerce platform might analyze chat transcripts to identify recurring issues, such as delayed responses or unclear policies. By addressing these pain points, the company enhances service quality and strengthens customer relationships. Feedback loops also enable proactive problem-solving, such as predicting customer dissatisfaction trends based on historical data and implementing preventative measures.

Even small-scale and individual applications of feedback loops can yield significant benefits. Freelancers and small business owners often use feedback loops to refine their offerings and improve client relationships. A graphic designer, for example, might seek client input at various stages of a project, ensuring alignment with expectations and avoiding rework. Similarly, a boutique café might use customer reviews to adjust menu offerings or service practices. These smaller-scale applications demonstrate the universality of feedback loops, proving their value in settings beyond large organizations.

Real-world applications of feedback loops showcase their adaptability and effectiveness across sectors. Whether optimizing assembly lines, improving patient care, developing software, or enhancing customer satisfaction, feedback loops empower organizations to evolve in response to challenges and opportunities. By embedding these iterative mechanisms into their processes, businesses of all sizes and industries can achieve continuous improvement, delivering better outcomes and fostering long-term success.

Leverage Technology to Streamline Repetitive Tasks

Incorporating technology into feedback loops is a powerful way to enhance efficiency, especially when addressing repetitive tasks. By automating data collection, analysis, and reporting, organizations can allocate human resources to more strategic and creative activities. Technology serves as both an enabler and accelerator, reducing the burden of manual intervention and ensuring that feedback loops remain timely, accurate, and actionable. The ability to streamline repetitive tasks using advanced tools has revolutionized industries, offering benefits that extend from improved productivity to more informed decision-making.

The first advantage of leveraging technology lies in its capacity to automate data collection. Traditional methods, such as manual surveys or paper-based logs, are often labor-intensive and prone to errors. In contrast, digital solutions like IoT sensors, CRM systems, and cloud-based platforms provide real-time data with minimal human oversight. For instance, in industrial settings, sensors can continuously monitor equipment performance, automatically flagging deviations from expected parameters. Similarly, customer feedback can be gathered seamlessly through online forms, app-based prompts, or even AI-driven chatbots. By automating these repetitive tasks, organizations ensure a steady flow of reliable data into their feedback loops.

Another key benefit of technology is its ability to enhance data analysis. Modern tools powered by artificial intelligence (AI) and machine learning (ML) can sift through vast datasets to identify patterns, trends, and anomalies that might be missed by human analysts. For example, an e-commerce platform using AI analytics can detect shifts in customer purchasing behavior, such as declining interest in a particular product category. This insight allows the company to adjust inventory levels or marketing strategies proactively. By automating repetitive analytical tasks, technology not only speeds up the feedback loop but also delivers deeper, more actionable insights.

Technology also plays a crucial role in facilitating timely and effective communication within feedback loops. Collaboration platforms like Slack, Microsoft Teams, and Trello integrate with feedback systems to ensure that relevant insights reach the right stakeholders promptly. Automated notifications, dashboards, and reporting tools reduce the lag between data collection and action. For instance, in IT project management, an integrated system might send an automated alert when a task falls behind schedule, enabling teams to address the issue immediately. This streamlined communication ensures that feedback loops remain dynamic, keeping processes on track and responsive to change.

Furthermore, technology can be leveraged to test and implement improvements derived from feedback loops. Simulation tools, digital twins, and A/B testing platforms allow organizations to experiment with changes in a controlled environment before rolling them out broadly. For instance, a retailer might use A/B testing to evaluate two variations of a promotional campaign, measuring which approach generates higher engagement. This iterative approach, supported by technology, minimizes risk while maximizing the impact of process refinements. The ability to experiment efficiently underscores the transformative potential of integrating technology into feedback loops.

Despite these advantages, the effective use of technology in feedback loops requires careful consideration. Organizations must select tools that align with their specific needs and ensure proper training for employees to maximize adoption and effectiveness. Additionally, ethical concerns related to data privacy and security must be addressed, particularly in industries like healthcare or finance where sensitive information is involved. By prioritizing these considerations, organizations can fully leverage technology while maintaining trust and compliance.

Technology serves as a critical enabler for streamlining repetitive tasks within feedback loops. By automating data collection, enhancing analysis, facilitating communication, and enabling controlled experimentation, technology transforms feedback loops into efficient, high-impact mechanisms for continuous improvement. When applied thoughtfully, these tools free up human talent for strategic initiatives, allowing organizations to innovate and adapt in an increasingly complex and competitive landscape.

DESIGNING SUSTAINABLE FEEDBACK LOOPS

Creating feedback loops that stand the test of time requires a focus on sustainability. Feedback systems often falter due to lack of maintenance, engagement, or adaptability, making their long-term viability a pressing concern. To ensure processes remain effective and relevant, organizations must design feedback loops with an emphasis on resilience, inclusivity, and adaptability to evolving needs. A sustainable feedback loop becomes not only a tool for improvement but also a self-sustaining mechanism that continuously fuels progress.

Sustainability begins with clarity of purpose. Feedback loops must be built with a clear understanding of their objectives and the outcomes they aim to achieve. For example, a feedback loop designed to improve employee performance should clearly define its parameters, such as measuring specific skills or behaviors and linking these to broader organizational goals. Without a focused purpose, feedback systems risk becoming convoluted or misaligned, reducing their impact over time. Ensuring that the loop remains purpose-driven provides a strong foundation for longevity.

Inclusivity is another cornerstone of sustainable feedback loops. Processes that exclude key stakeholders—whether employees, customers, or external partners—are less likely to remain effective. A robust feedback system actively engages diverse perspectives, fostering a sense of ownership and collaboration among participants. For instance, a retail company seeking to enhance customer satisfaction might involve employees at all levels, from frontline staff who interact directly with customers to management who oversee operations. By incorporating multiple viewpoints, the feedback loop captures a richer dataset and garners broader buy-in, making it more durable over time.

Adaptability is essential for a feedback loop to stay relevant. Static systems that fail to evolve with changing circumstances quickly lose their effectiveness. To address this, feedback loops should be designed with mechanisms that allow for regular review and adjustment. For example, an IT company using a feedback loop to improve software development might incorporate periodic retrospectives, where teams assess the loop's performance and refine its elements. This iterative approach ensures the system remains aligned with current challenges and opportunities, maintaining its utility in a dynamic environment.

Technology also plays a pivotal role in sustaining feedback loops. Automation tools, real-time data analytics, and AI-driven platforms can help reduce the manual effort required to maintain feedback systems. For instance, a logistics company might use IoT sensors to monitor fleet performance, feeding data into an automated loop that identifies inefficiencies and suggests adjustments. By reducing the reliance on human intervention for repetitive tasks, technology enhances the sustainability of feedback loops, allowing organizations to focus on higher-order improvements.

Embedding feedback loops into organizational culture solidifies their sustainability. When feedback is treated as an occasional exercise rather than an ongoing practice, it risks being sidelined during periods of crisis or change. Organizations that weave feedback into their daily operations—such as by encouraging open dialogue, rewarding participation, and integrating loops into performance metrics—are more likely to see these systems endure. For example, a company that fosters a culture of psychological safety, where employees feel comfortable sharing honest feedback, creates fertile ground for sustainable improvement processes.

By focusing on clarity, inclusivity, adaptability, technological integration, and cultural embedding, organizations can design feedback loops that endure. These systems become more than just tools for refinement—they evolve into dynamic frameworks that continuously adapt and grow with the organization, driving ongoing success. The ability to sustain feedback loops is not only a strategic advantage but also a testament to an organization's commitment to excellence and resilience.

THE TRANSFORMATIVE POWER OF FEEDBACK LOOPS

Feedback loops possess a remarkable ability to reshape organizations, industries, and even individual behaviors. Their transformative potential lies in their capacity to foster continuous learning, enhance decision-making, and adapt processes to meet evolving demands. Far beyond being mere tools for refinement, feedback loops are dynamic systems that can catalyze profound change when implemented with intentionality and foresight.

At the heart of their transformative power is the principle of continuous learning. Feedback loops establish an ongoing cycle where insights drive improvements, which in turn generate new insights, creating a perpetual state of growth and refinement. For example, in the tech sector, agile development thrives on iterative feedback loops. Each software release is informed by user feedback, leading to enhancements that directly address customer needs. This process not only improves the product but also fosters a culture of responsiveness and innovation, demonstrating how feedback loops can transform both outcomes and organizational mindsets.

Feedback loops also enhance decision-making by providing data-driven insights that reduce uncertainty. In environments where decisions must be made quickly and with limited information, feedback loops serve as a critical compass. Consider a supply chain disrupted by global events: companies with robust feedback mechanisms can rapidly assess delays, identify bottlenecks, and implement alternative solutions. By continuously feeding real-time information into decision-making processes, feedback loops transform reactive responses into proactive strategies, allowing organizations to navigate complexity with confidence.

Another transformative aspect of feedback loops is their ability to align diverse stakeholders toward common goals. By ensuring that input flows seamlessly between different levels of an organization, feedback loops break down silos and foster collaboration. For instance, a healthcare system aiming to improve patient care might implement feedback loops that integrate perspectives from patients, clinicians, and administrative staff. This holistic approach ensures that changes are informed by a comprehensive understanding of the system, leading to solutions that are both effective and equitable. The transformation here is not just operational but also cultural, as collaboration becomes a core organizational value.

The adaptability inherent in feedback loops makes them powerful agents of change in dynamic environments. Unlike rigid processes that struggle to keep pace with shifting circumstances, feedback loops are inherently flexible, allowing organizations to pivot and evolve. This adaptability is particularly evident in industries like e-commerce, where consumer preferences change rapidly. Companies that integrate real-time feedback into their marketing and inventory strategies can anticipate trends and adjust offerings before competitors, transforming their ability to remain relevant and competitive in volatile markets.

Perhaps most significantly, feedback loops empower individuals and organizations to achieve breakthroughs that might otherwise remain elusive. By continuously challenging assumptions, highlighting inefficiencies, and surfacing new opportunities, feedback loops drive innovation at every level. For example, in education, teachers using feedback loops to adapt lesson plans based on student performance can tailor their approaches to meet diverse learning needs, transforming the classroom experience and improving outcomes for students. Similarly, startups leveraging customer feedback to refine their business models often discover untapped markets or unique value propositions that set them apart.

The transformative power of feedback loops extends beyond operational improvements; it reshapes mindsets and fosters resilience. By embracing feedback as a source of growth rather than criticism, individuals and organizations cultivate a willingness to experiment, take risks, and learn from failure. This shift in perspective is a hallmark of innovative cultures and is central to long-term success. Feedback loops become not just mechanisms for change but also symbols of adaptability, learning, and progress.

Feedback loops are transformative because they integrate learning, enhance decision-making, foster collaboration, enable adaptability, and drive innovation. When embraced fully, they unlock potential that goes beyond the immediate benefits of process refinement, positioning individuals and organizations to thrive in an ever-changing world. Their power lies in their simplicity and scalability, proving that even the most straightforward mechanisms, when applied with intention, can lead to extraordinary outcomes.

Case studies of organizations that transformed through procedural innovation

Procedural innovation represents one of the most impactful ways organizations can achieve lasting transformation. It involves rethinking and redesigning the processes that govern how work is done, often with the goal of improving efficiency, fostering creativity, and aligning with strategic goals. While the concept may sound abstract, its effects are vividly tangible, shaping industries, redefining customer expectations, and driving growth in ways that are both measurable and profound. To truly understand its potential, one must look beyond theory and into the real-world examples of organizations that have embraced procedural innovation to revolutionize their operations and outcomes.

Case studies are uniquely powerful in showcasing the practical application and results of procedural innovation. They reveal not only the successes but also the challenges and complexities inherent in implementing change. Unlike generic frameworks or theoretical models, case studies provide a narrative—a story of transformation that highlights the decisions, obstacles, and adaptations involved. By examining these examples, readers gain a nuanced understanding of what procedural innovation looks like in practice, including the critical factors that contribute to its success or failure.

Another compelling aspect of case studies is their ability to highlight the diversity of contexts in which procedural innovation can thrive. Whether in manufacturing, healthcare, e-commerce, or entertainment, the principles of process refinement and creativity can be tailored to vastly different industries. This diversity underscores a universal truth: procedural innovation is not confined to specific sectors or organizations but is a versatile tool capable of addressing challenges and unlocking opportunities across all areas of business activity.

Additionally, studying real-world examples helps to demystify the process of procedural innovation, making it feel accessible and achievable. It is easy to perceive major organizational transformations as the result of visionary leadership or unique circumstances. However, case studies often reveal that these changes are rooted in methodical adjustments to how work is done—changes that are informed by feedback, driven by collaboration, and guided by a clear understanding of goals. This revelation empowers individuals and teams to see procedural innovation as something they can actively pursue, regardless of their role or resources.

Finally, the examination of case studies serves as a reminder of the potential for continuous learning and improvement. By analyzing how other organizations have navigated the terrain of procedural innovation, readers can draw lessons that resonate with their own challenges and aspirations. These stories provide a source of inspiration, showing that transformation is not only possible but also a natural outcome of thoughtful, deliberate change. Through this lens, procedural innovation becomes more than a theoretical concept—it becomes a practical, actionable pathway to growth and success.

In this chapter, we will explore organizations that have embraced procedural innovation to redefine their industries and achieve extraordinary results. Each example will illuminate the challenges they faced, the innovative processes they implemented, and the outcomes they achieved. These stories will not only inform but also inspire, illustrating the profound impact of procedural innovation on businesses, industries, and even broader societal systems.

Case Study 1: The Transformation of Toyota through Lean Manufacturing

Toyota's journey from a struggling automaker in post-war Japan to a global leader in manufacturing excellence is a masterclass in procedural innovation. The introduction of the Toyota Production System (TPS), rooted in the principles of Lean Manufacturing, transformed the company's operations and reshaped the entire automotive industry. Essentially, this transformation was driven by a commitment to process improvement, efficiency, and the elimination of waste, all of which underscored the profound impact that well-designed procedures can have on organizational success.

In the 1940s, Toyota faced immense challenges. The Japanese economy was in recovery mode after the war, resources were scarce, and the company needed to find a way to compete with established Western automakers. Conventional mass production methods, which focused on high output and large inventories, were not viable in this resource-constrained environment. Toyota's leadership recognized that they needed a fundamentally different approach—one that maximized efficiency without sacrificing quality. This realization marked the genesis of the TPS, which introduced groundbreaking procedural innovations designed to optimize every stage of production.

The TPS was built on two foundational pillars: *just-in-time* (JIT) production and *jidoka* (automation with a human touch). JIT emphasized producing only what was needed, when it was needed, and in the quantity required, reducing waste and minimizing excess inventory. Jidoka, on the other hand, allowed machines to automatically stop when a problem occurred, enabling workers to address issues immediately. These principles were not merely technical adjustments; they represented a profound shift in how work was structured and how teams operated. Workers became empowered participants in the process, responsible for maintaining quality and suggesting improvements, fostering a culture of continuous innovation.

The impact of these procedural changes was transformative. Toyota's production times and costs decreased significantly, while quality and reliability improved. These advantages allowed the company to compete on a global scale, gaining a reputation for producing vehicles of unmatched durability and efficiency. Over time, the principles of Lean Manufacturing spread beyond Toyota, influencing industries as diverse as healthcare, software development, and retail. The term "Lean" became synonymous with operational excellence, underscoring Toyota's role as a pioneer in procedural innovation.

For readers, Toyota's story offers valuable lessons that extend beyond manufacturing. At its heart, the success of the TPS lies in its adaptability and its focus on aligning processes with organizational goals. Toyota demonstrated that procedural innovation is not about rigid adherence to rules but about creating systems that are responsive, efficient, and sustainable. This case study illustrates the power of embracing a mindset of continuous improvement, where every team member contributes to refining and optimizing processes. It also highlights the importance of challenging conventional approaches, showing that groundbreaking innovation often emerges from necessity and resourcefulness.

Toyota's transformation serves as a blueprint for organizations seeking to enhance their operations through procedural innovation. It shows that even in the face of significant constraints, rethinking how work is done can unlock extraordinary potential. By fostering a culture of collaboration, adaptability, and problem-solving, businesses can replicate Toyota's success, not only in terms of efficiency but also in building a legacy of innovation and excellence.

CASE STUDY 2: AMAZON'S PROCEDURAL REINVENTION IN SUPPLY CHAIN MANAGEMENT

Amazon's rise from an online bookseller to a global e-commerce titan is a testament to its mastery of supply chain management, driven by continuous procedural innovation. At the heart of Amazon's success lies its ability to streamline complex logistical processes while remaining adaptable to evolving consumer demands. Through relentless refinement of its supply chain procedures, Amazon has set new benchmarks for speed, efficiency, and customer satisfaction, redefining how goods are bought and delivered worldwide.

In its early years, Amazon relied on traditional fulfillment practices, outsourcing many aspects of its logistics. However, as the company grew, it became evident that conventional approaches were insufficient to meet its ambitious goals of offering vast product selections, competitive pricing, and fast delivery. Recognizing the need for transformation, Amazon began to reinvent its supply chain by investing in advanced technologies, proprietary systems, and innovative processes. This procedural reinvention was not incremental but systemic, addressing every aspect of the supply chain—from inventory management and warehousing to delivery and customer service.

One of Amazon's most significant innovations was the development of its fulfillment center model, which introduced unprecedented levels of efficiency and scalability. These centers operate on a meticulously designed process where advanced robotics and artificial intelligence (AI) work alongside human employees to optimize the storage, retrieval, and packaging of goods. Items are stored in randomized locations rather than traditional categorical arrangements, a method known as "chaotic storage." This approach, powered by AI algorithms, significantly reduces retrieval time and maximizes storage capacity. The integration of automation and data-driven decision-making exemplifies how procedural innovation can transform traditionally labor-intensive tasks into highly efficient operations.

Another groundbreaking advancement was the introduction of Amazon Prime and its promise of two-day—and later same-day—delivery. Achieving this required rethinking the last-mile delivery process. Amazon developed its proprietary logistics network, including a fleet of delivery vehicles, partnerships with local couriers, and even experimentation with drones. By vertically integrating its delivery operations, Amazon reduced dependency on external carriers, gained greater control over timelines, and enhanced reliability. These procedural enhancements not only improved operational efficiency but also became a cornerstone of Amazon's competitive advantage, fostering customer loyalty and setting new standards for the industry.

Beyond logistics, Amazon's supply chain innovation extends to its use of predictive analytics and machine learning to manage inventory and anticipate demand. By analyzing vast amounts of data, Amazon can forecast purchasing patterns, minimize overstocking, and ensure high-demand items are readily available. This level of precision underscores the importance of leveraging technology in procedural innovation, as it enables companies to adapt dynamically to market fluctuations and customer expectations.

For organizations seeking to emulate Amazon's success, this case study highlights several critical takeaways. First, procedural innovation requires a willingness to challenge conventional wisdom and adopt unconventional methods, such as chaotic storage. Second, the integration of technology is essential for scaling processes while maintaining flexibility. Finally, a customer-centric approach, as exemplified by Amazon Prime, ensures that procedural improvements align with broader business objectives and deliver tangible value to end-users.

Amazon's reinvention of supply chain management demonstrates the transformative power of procedural innovation in creating systems that are both efficient and adaptable. By continually refining its processes and embracing a culture of experimentation, Amazon has not only sustained its competitive edge but also redefined industry standards, offering a blueprint for organizations aiming to achieve operational excellence.

Case Study 3: Mayo Clinic's Integration of Standardized Medical Procedures

The Mayo Clinic, one of the world's most respected healthcare institutions, owes much of its success to its innovative use of standardized medical procedures. In an industry where errors can be life-threatening and efficiency can mean the difference between life and death, the Mayo Clinic has exemplified how procedural innovation can harmonize complex operations, enhance patient care, and foster collaboration among medical professionals. By combining rigorous standardization with a patient-centered approach, the Mayo Clinic has redefined healthcare excellence.

Historically, healthcare has been a field where variability in practices is common due to differences in training, experience, and regional protocols. Recognizing the risks this posed, the Mayo Clinic adopted a model emphasizing standardized procedures as early as the 20th century. This approach was grounded in the idea that uniformity in processes would reduce errors, ensure consistent quality of care, and allow for seamless collaboration among medical professionals. For instance, the clinic was one of the first to implement detailed procedural checklists for surgeries and complex medical treatments, long before such practices became industry standards.

One key innovation was the integration of multidisciplinary teams into the procedural workflow. Unlike many hospitals where specialists operate in silos, the Mayo Clinic designed a system where professionals from various disciplines collaborate on each patient's care. This process relies heavily on standardized protocols to ensure that every team member is aligned, from initial diagnosis to treatment plans and follow-up care. These protocols not only streamline communication but also enable the clinic to deliver holistic and coordinated care, which has been shown to improve patient outcomes significantly.

Another area of procedural innovation at the Mayo Clinic is its use of data-driven decision-making. The institution has developed and refined processes for collecting and analyzing patient data to guide treatment. For example, the Clinic's adoption of electronic health records (EHRs) and integration of predictive analytics have transformed how doctors approach diagnosis and treatment planning. By embedding these tools within standardized workflows, the Mayo Clinic ensures that physicians have access to real-time, evidence-based insights, reducing variability in care and enhancing decision-making.

A particularly impactful example of procedural standardization is the Mayo Clinic's approach to surgical safety. By implementing comprehensive preoperative checklists, the Clinic reduced surgical complications and mortality rates. These checklists, which are now widely adopted across the healthcare industry, ensure that every step of the process—from verifying patient information to reviewing potential risks—is conducted meticulously. This procedural rigor not only enhances patient safety but also fosters a culture of accountability and teamwork among medical staff.

For organizations outside healthcare, the Mayo Clinic offers a powerful lesson in the value of procedural standardization without sacrificing innovation or adaptability. By designing processes that prioritize collaboration, data utilization, and continuous improvement, the Clinic demonstrates how standardization can be a catalyst for excellence rather than a constraint. It underscores the importance of aligning procedures with the ultimate goal—in this case, patient care—and ensuring that every team member understands and contributes to the process.

The Mayo Clinic's integration of standardized medical procedures highlights the transformative potential of aligning meticulous planning with a commitment to innovation. By reducing variability, enhancing collaboration, and embedding data-driven insights into workflows, the Clinic has created a system that not only sustains operational excellence but also serves as a benchmark for quality and efficiency in healthcare. This case study offers inspiration for any organization seeking to leverage procedural innovation to achieve consistently exceptional outcomes.

Case Study 3: Mayo Clinic's Integration of Standardized Medical Procedures

The Mayo Clinic, consistently ranked as one of the top medical institutions in the world, owes much of its success to its integration of standardized medical procedures. In an environment as complex and high-stakes as healthcare, variability in practice can lead to errors, inefficiencies, and inequitable patient outcomes. By innovating around procedural standardization while maintaining a patient-first philosophy, the Mayo Clinic has set a global benchmark for delivering safe, efficient, and collaborative medical care.

One of the cornerstone achievements of the Mayo Clinic has been its early recognition of the need for procedural consistency in multidisciplinary care. The institution embraced a team-based approach where specialists from diverse fields work together seamlessly. This collaboration relies on standardized workflows that ensure every team member contributes effectively at each stage of patient care. For example, the clinic developed a model where diagnoses, treatment plans, and follow-ups are systematically discussed in team meetings. These processes ensure that patient care is comprehensive, evidence-based, and devoid of unnecessary redundancies or delays.

The adoption of clinical protocols, such as preoperative and postoperative guidelines, further exemplifies the Clinic's commitment to procedural standardization. Long before surgical safety checklists became standard practice worldwide, the Mayo Clinic implemented meticulous protocols to ensure patient safety during operations. From verifying patient identity and surgical site to ensuring post-surgical recovery protocols were uniformly applied, these processes reduced the likelihood of errors and enhanced surgical outcomes. These protocols have since inspired global safety initiatives, including those spearheaded by the World Health Organization (WHO).

Data-driven innovation is another critical component of the Mayo Clinic's procedural excellence. The institution has invested heavily in electronic health records (EHRs) and predictive analytics systems to refine its workflows. By embedding these tools within standardized processes, medical teams have access to real-time data and insights that guide their decisions. For instance, predictive algorithms help identify patients at risk of complications, enabling early interventions. This combination of technology and procedural rigor exemplifies how standardization can enhance adaptability and responsiveness in dynamic environments.

Perhaps the most profound impact of the Mayo Clinic's procedural innovations is its cultural influence. The emphasis on consistency and collaboration has cultivated a workplace ethos where patient outcomes take precedence over individual achievements. Physicians and staff are trained to adhere to the highest procedural standards while remaining open to continuous learning and improvement. This dual focus on procedure and adaptability has allowed the Mayo Clinic to stay at the forefront of medical innovation while maintaining the trust and loyalty of its patients.

The Mayo Clinic's procedural framework is a model for organizations seeking to balance efficiency with excellence. By demonstrating how standardized processes can coexist with cutting-edge innovation, it challenges the misconception that standardization stifles creativity. Instead, it proves that well-designed procedures serve as a foundation for adaptability, collaboration, and sustained success. For industries beyond healthcare, the Mayo Clinic stands as a testament to the transformative potential of aligning procedural rigor with a commitment to continuous improvement.

The Common Threads in Procedural Innovation

Procedural innovation, while often tailored to the specific needs and challenges of an organization, reveals recurring themes that transcend industries and contexts. These common threads highlight the principles and strategies that underpin successful transformations. By examining these shared elements, organizations can better understand how to implement and sustain innovative procedures in their unique environments.

One prevalent theme is the alignment of procedures with organizational goals. Whether it's Toyota's focus on lean efficiency, Amazon's dedication to customer satisfaction, or the Mayo Clinic's commitment to patient care, successful procedural innovations are always anchored in a clear and overarching mission. This alignment ensures that procedures are not imposed as arbitrary rules but are perceived as tools for achieving meaningful objectives. It also provides a guiding framework for decision-making during the innovation process, helping organizations prioritize actions that contribute to their core mission.

Another shared element is the emphasis on data and feedback as drivers of procedural refinement. Across industries, data serves as the lifeblood of innovation, revealing inefficiencies, identifying opportunities, and tracking progress. Feedback loops, whether they involve customer reviews, employee input, or real-time analytics, allow organizations to iterate on their processes continuously. The Mayo Clinic's use of predictive analytics in medical procedures, for instance, exemplifies how data integration can elevate procedural outcomes by providing actionable insights at every stage.

Collaboration emerges as another fundamental thread in procedural innovation. Whether it's cross-disciplinary teams in healthcare, integrated supply chain management in retail, or production floor collaboration in manufacturing, successful procedural innovation requires collective effort. Open communication, shared accountability, and mutual respect among team members foster an environment where ideas can be exchanged freely, and improvements are embraced. This collaborative approach not only strengthens the innovation process but also ensures greater buy-in from stakeholders who feel invested in the changes.

Adaptability within structure is another key principle that surfaces repeatedly. Procedural innovation often involves striking a delicate balance between maintaining order and allowing flexibility. Organizations like Toyota, Amazon, and the Mayo Clinic have demonstrated the power of embedding adaptability into their standardized processes. By creating frameworks that accommodate evolving needs—whether through modular workflows, scalable systems, or continuous learning mechanisms—these organizations ensure that their procedures remain relevant in dynamic environments.

The culture of continuous improvement ties all these threads together. The most successful examples of procedural innovation stem from organizations that view processes as living systems rather than static rules. This mindset fosters a culture where experimentation is encouraged, mistakes are seen as learning opportunities, and every individual feels empowered to contribute to procedural excellence. Such a culture not only sustains the momentum of innovation but also creates an enduring competitive advantage for organizations willing to evolve.

The common threads in procedural innovation underscore the universality of certain principles while allowing for contextual customization. By aligning procedures with goals, leveraging data and feedback, fostering collaboration, ensuring adaptability, and cultivating a culture of improvement, organizations can create systems that not only enhance efficiency but also drive transformative success. These lessons serve as a blueprint for any entity seeking to harness the power of procedural innovation, regardless of its industry or scale.

ACTIONABLE INSIGHTS FOR IMPLEMENTING PROCEDURAL INNOVATION

Transforming procedures to foster innovation requires a pragmatic approach that combines strategic planning with active execution. While high-level concepts like collaboration and adaptability are vital, they must translate into tangible actions to drive meaningful change. The following actionable insights provide a roadmap for organizations seeking to implement procedural innovation effectively, ensuring that efforts lead to sustained improvements.

One of the first steps in procedural innovation is conducting a thorough assessment of existing processes. Organizations should map out workflows to identify bottlenecks, redundancies, and inefficiencies. This exercise often uncovers areas where procedures are misaligned with current objectives or create unnecessary complexity. For instance, leveraging tools like process flowcharts or value stream mapping can help teams visualize where delays or errors occur. By analyzing these gaps, organizations can prioritize which procedures require immediate redesign and focus resources accordingly.

Equally crucial is engaging stakeholders at every level during the innovation process. Employees, managers, and external partners who interact with procedures daily often hold valuable insights into what works and what doesn't. Encouraging open dialogue through workshops, surveys, or brainstorming sessions ensures that procedural changes address real pain points and gain widespread support. For example, Amazon's success in supply chain innovation was partly due to its inclusive approach, where warehouse workers and logistics managers contributed ideas for streamlining operations. Collaboration at this stage fosters a sense of ownership and reduces resistance to change.

Technology integration is another key driver of procedural innovation. Advanced tools like automation software, artificial intelligence, and predictive analytics can simplify complex tasks, enhance decision-making, and reduce errors. Organizations should focus on adopting technologies that align with their unique needs rather than pursuing trends without a clear strategy. For example, implementing an enterprise resource planning (ERP) system can unify various processes under one platform, improving visibility and coordination across departments. However, technology should complement human effort, with employees trained to leverage tools effectively rather than being overshadowed by them.

To sustain innovation, organizations must embed feedback loops within their procedures. Regularly scheduled evaluations—whether through performance metrics, employee feedback, or customer reviews—ensure that processes remain relevant and effective over time. For example, a hospital adopting standardized surgical protocols might use post-operative data to identify variations in patient recovery times. This feedback can guide adjustments to protocols, ensuring continuous refinement. Without such loops, even the most innovative procedures risk becoming outdated or ineffective in changing environments.

Encouraging a culture of experimentation and learning is essential for procedural innovation to thrive. Organizations should encourage teams to test new approaches on a small scale before full implementation, using pilot programs or prototypes. This iterative approach minimizes risks while allowing for adjustments based on real-world outcomes. Leaders play a critical role in this process by creating a safe environment where failures are seen as opportunities for growth. For example, Toyota's Kaizen philosophy emphasizes continuous improvement through incremental changes, empowering employees at all levels to suggest and test innovations.

By following these actionable insights, organizations can transform their procedures into dynamic systems that drive efficiency, adaptability, and growth. The path to procedural innovation is not without challenges, but with clear steps and a commitment to improvement, businesses can unlock their full potential and create lasting value for all stakeholders.

Becoming a Procedural Champion

Procedures often seem like top-down mandates, shaped exclusively by leadership or specialized teams. However, this perception undermines the transformative potential of individuals at every level of an organization. The truth is, even the most effective processes thrive on contributions from those who engage with them daily. Each individual, regardless of their title or role, possesses the capacity to influence and refine these structures in meaningful ways. This principle lies at the heart of democratizing procedural excellence, emphasizing that impactful change begins with everyday actions and insights. Recognizing and harnessing this potential is the first step toward unlocking the collective strength of an organization.

History offers powerful examples of how individuals can catalyze significant change. Consider the case of Toyota's famous *kaizen* philosophy, where assembly-line workers are empowered to halt production lines if they identify inefficiencies or quality issues. This radical shift from rigid hierarchies to collaborative improvement revolutionized manufacturing, proving that procedural innovation can originate from the ground up. Whether it's a frontline employee suggesting a quicker filing system or a nurse proposing a safer medication delivery process, these contributions are often born from hands-on experience, offering perspectives that top-level designers may overlook. This highlights the dual truth: procedures are most effective when they are not just imposed but are actively shaped by those who live them.

Individual impact on procedures doesn't merely improve outcomes; it strengthens a sense of ownership and accountability. When individuals feel they have a voice in shaping processes, they become more invested in the success of those systems. This fosters a culture of collaboration where employees are motivated not just to follow the rules but to improve them. For instance, a marketing team member who devises a more streamlined client feedback process benefits not only the team but also develops personal skills such as problem-solving and project ownership. In turn, this sense of empowerment translates into enhanced job satisfaction and performance, creating a ripple effect across the organization.

The idea of individual influence also serves as a counterbalance to procedural stagnation. Over time, even the most well-designed processes risk becoming outdated as industries evolve and new challenges arise. Organizations that fail to encourage grassroots contributions risk becoming rigid, stifling innovation and adaptability. By contrast, companies that celebrate individual contributions to procedural evolution remain dynamic and competitive. A recent study in agile management practices shows that employee-led process improvements increase both efficiency and morale, reinforcing the idea that sustainable systems are co-created rather than merely dictated.

Embracing the power of individual impact reshapes the narrative around procedures themselves. Rather than being seen as static or constrictive, procedures become living entities—adaptable, responsive, and inclusive. This shift requires leaders to actively cultivate environments where contributions are not just accepted but encouraged and rewarded. Whether through formal feedback mechanisms or informal team discussions, opportunities for individual input transform processes from an abstract framework into a shared endeavor. When individuals see their insights recognized and implemented, the organizational benefits are profound: stronger systems, engaged employees, and a culture of continuous improvement.

MINDSETS FOR DRIVING PROCEDURAL EXCELLENCE

At the heart of any effort to enhance work procedures lies the mindset of those involved. Procedural excellence requires more than technical skills or industry knowledge; it demands a way of thinking that embraces adaptability, collaboration, and innovation. While procedures are often viewed as rigid structures, the most successful systems are born from flexible and forward-thinking mindsets. By fostering these mental frameworks, individuals and organizations can transform processes into powerful tools for growth, creativity, and sustained success.

A foundational mindset for procedural excellence is proactive ownership. This involves approaching procedures not as fixed instructions to follow passively but as dynamic systems open to improvement. Those with this mindset don't wait for permission to identify inefficiencies or propose changes—they take initiative. For example, an employee in a customer service role might notice recurring complaints that stem from an outdated response template. Rather than ignoring the issue or assuming someone else will address it, they develop and suggest a revised approach. This willingness to take responsibility for procedural outcomes fosters a culture where continuous improvement is valued over mere compliance.

Equally critical is adopting a growth mentality, which frames processes as evolving tools rather than static entities. Individuals with this mindset understand that what works today may not suffice tomorrow. They remain open to change, viewing procedural challenges as opportunities to learn and innovate. This perspective is especially valuable in industries undergoing rapid transformation, such as technology or healthcare. For instance, a software developer working within a rigid Agile framework might identify bottlenecks during sprints. By suggesting modifications tailored to the team's specific needs, they embody the belief that even well-established methods can benefit from refinement. This mindset prevents stagnation, ensuring that procedures remain relevant and effective over time.

Another essential mindset is empathy and collaboration. Procedures often intersect with diverse roles, departments, or stakeholders, each bringing unique priorities and constraints. To drive procedural excellence, individuals must consider how processes impact others and seek alignment across these varying perspectives. A procurement manager, for example, might notice delays caused by overly complex approval workflows. Instead of making unilateral changes, they engage with colleagues in finance and operations to co-create a streamlined system that meets everyone's needs. This empathetic approach not only improves outcomes but also builds trust and cooperation among teams, ensuring that procedural changes are embraced rather than resisted.

The mindset of resilience in the face of resistance is equally vital. Procedural improvements, particularly those initiated from the ground up, often encounter skepticism or opposition. Navigating these challenges requires persistence and a belief in the value of one's contributions. A junior team member proposing a new project tracking method might face initial pushback from senior colleagues accustomed to traditional systems. However, by presenting clear evidence of the new method's benefits and patiently addressing concerns, they can gradually win support. This mindset ensures that valuable ideas are not abandoned prematurely but are given the chance to demonstrate their impact.

Encouraging a mindset of shared accountability elevates procedural excellence from an individual effort to a collective pursuit. When individuals recognize their role in shaping and sustaining processes, they move beyond a "not my job" mentality to one of active engagement. This requires creating environments where contributions are acknowledged and rewarded, reinforcing the belief that everyone has a stake in procedural success. By embedding these mindsets into workplace culture, organizations can unlock the full potential of their people, transforming procedures into living systems that reflect the creativity, collaboration, and resilience of those who drive them.

SKILLS FOR ENHANCING WORK PROCEDURES

While a proactive mindset forms the foundation for procedural excellence, its realization requires a set of practical skills. These competencies enable individuals to identify inefficiencies, design effective solutions, and collaborate with others to implement meaningful change. Whether working in an executive role or as an entry-level team member, developing these skills equips individuals to actively contribute to and enhance the work procedures that define organizational success.

The first essential skill is process analysis, which involves breaking down existing workflows to identify areas of inefficiency, redundancy, or inconsistency. This requires a keen eye for detail and the ability to evaluate processes holistically. For instance, a logistics coordinator may analyze a shipping procedure and uncover delays caused by insufficient inventory checks. By documenting the process step by step and identifying bottlenecks, they can recommend adjustments that improve efficiency and reliability. Process analysis is not merely about identifying flaws; it's about understanding the interplay of various components and finding opportunities for optimization.

Closely linked to analysis is the ability to design and document procedures clearly and concisely. A well-designed process minimizes ambiguity and ensures that team members across roles can follow it consistently. This skill involves not only technical writing but also an understanding of how people interact with instructions. Consider a project manager revising an onboarding procedure. Beyond outlining tasks, they use visual aids like flowcharts and templates to simplify the steps for new hires. Effective documentation reduces errors and fosters a shared understanding of expectations, enabling smooth and scalable operations.

Another critical skill is communication and facilitation, particularly in the context of collaborative environments. Procedural changes often require buy-in from multiple stakeholders, and facilitating productive discussions is key to achieving alignment. This involves presenting ideas persuasively, addressing concerns, and incorporating feedback to create solutions that resonate with all parties. For example, a healthcare administrator proposing changes to patient intake procedures might host a series of workshops with doctors, nurses, and reception staff to ensure their needs are addressed. By fostering open dialogue, they build consensus and pave the way for successful implementation.

The ability to leverage technology and tools is increasingly indispensable in modern procedural improvement. From project management software to automation platforms, technological tools can streamline workflows, enhance data accuracy, and reduce manual effort. However, the skill lies not just in using these tools but in selecting the right ones for the task at hand and integrating them seamlessly into existing systems. For instance, a marketing specialist might adopt customer relationship management (CRM) software to track leads more effectively. By configuring the tool to align with the team's specific needs, they ensure it enhances rather than complicates daily operations.

The skill of adaptive problem-solving is crucial for navigating the complexities of procedural refinement. This involves thinking creatively and strategically to address challenges, particularly when ideal solutions are not immediately apparent. For example, a manufacturing supervisor may need to revise a production schedule to meet increased demand without compromising quality. By analyzing available resources, testing alternative approaches, and iterating on solutions, they develop a flexible plan that achieves the desired outcome. Adaptive problem-solving not only resolves immediate issues but also fosters resilience in the face of future challenges.

By cultivating these skills, individuals position themselves as valuable contributors to procedural excellence. More than technical competencies, these abilities embody the creativity, collaboration, and precision necessary to create systems that drive organizational success. When applied consistently, these skills empower individuals to transform abstract ideas into actionable, sustainable improvements, benefiting both their teams and the broader organization.

STRATEGIES TO CONTRIBUTE REGARDLESS OF ROLE

Contributing to procedural excellence is not reserved for leadership positions or specialized roles. Regardless of one's title or place within an organization, there are actionable strategies that individuals can adopt to influence work procedures positively. By leveraging curiosity, initiative, and collaboration, employees at every level can participate in creating systems that drive efficiency and innovation, demonstrating that impactful contributions stem from effort and creativity rather than authority alone.

The first strategy is to observe and engage with existing procedures actively. Every process, no matter how well-defined, carries subtle inefficiencies or areas ripe for improvement. By immersing themselves in daily operations, individuals can identify pain points that might escape formal audits or managerial oversight. For example, a customer support agent might notice recurring complaints stemming from unclear return policies. By documenting these patterns and suggesting a streamlined resolution, they highlight how small insights can lead to significant procedural enhancements. Active engagement signals a commitment to improvement and reinforces the idea that even minor observations can have meaningful impacts.

Another impactful approach is to propose small, incremental changes rather than overhauling entire systems. Sweeping procedural reforms can be intimidating and difficult to implement, especially without formal authority. Instead, employees can focus on suggesting manageable adjustments that address immediate concerns or inefficiencies. For instance, a team member working in a warehouse might recommend reordering inventory shelves based on frequency of use to minimize retrieval time. These smaller changes are easier to execute and can demonstrate the value of procedural refinement, building momentum for more extensive improvements over time.

Collaboration serves as another cornerstone strategy for contributing to better procedures. Building alliances and soliciting diverse input ensures that procedural changes are both effective and widely supported. Employees can form informal working groups or partner with colleagues from different departments to brainstorm solutions. For example, an IT specialist tasked with updating internal software can collaborate with end-users from HR or accounting to ensure the changes address practical challenges. Engaging others not only enriches the quality of proposed solutions but also fosters a sense of shared ownership, making the adoption of new procedures smoother and more inclusive.

The strategy of leveraging feedback loops is equally vital in contributing to procedural improvement. Soliciting and acting on feedback transforms passive compliance into active collaboration. This involves both seeking input on current processes and sharing insights with peers and supervisors. For example, a junior analyst could survey colleagues to understand frustrations with data entry workflows, compiling their suggestions into a comprehensive report for the team. By positioning feedback as an iterative tool, individuals can ensure that procedures evolve continuously rather than remaining static. Feedback loops also reinforce transparency, fostering a culture where all contributions are valued.

Individuals can contribute by championing a culture of experimentation and learning. Encouraging a mindset where trial and error are embraced allows teams to test new methods without fear of failure. Even without formal leadership roles, employees can advocate for pilot programs or experiments that refine workflows. For instance, a sales associate might propose testing a new scheduling app on a small scale before rolling it out company-wide. By taking ownership of these experiments and evaluating their outcomes, individuals demonstrate initiative and a willingness to innovate. This strategy not only refines processes but also inspires colleagues to adopt a similarly proactive stance.

These strategies illustrate that procedural excellence is accessible to all, regardless of role or title. By observing, collaborating, and advocating for change, individuals can position themselves as integral contributors to their organization's success. More importantly, these contributions reaffirm that the power to shape effective systems lies within everyone's reach, transforming work procedures into tools for collective achievement.

BUILDING CREDIBILITY AS A PROCEDURAL CONTRIBUTOR

Credibility is a cornerstone of effective contributions to work procedures, especially when one lacks formal authority. It ensures that ideas are taken seriously, considered objectively, and implemented with confidence. Building credibility as a procedural contributor requires a combination of consistent performance, relationship-building, and the ability to communicate ideas persuasively. By cultivating a reputation for reliability and insight, individuals can influence procedures and foster a culture of continuous improvement within their organizations.

The foundation of credibility lies in demonstrating a strong understanding of existing procedures and organizational goals. Employees who take the time to master the systems they work within naturally position themselves as knowledgeable contributors. This includes familiarizing themselves with not just how procedures are executed but also why they exist. For instance, understanding that a certain step in a workflow mitigates compliance risks makes it easier to suggest alternatives that achieve the same purpose with greater efficiency. By showing an appreciation for the broader context, contributors signal that their ideas are rooted in a deep understanding of both operational and strategic priorities.

Another critical aspect of building credibility is delivering consistent, high-quality work within one's current role. Credibility begins with reliability; people are more likely to trust suggestions from individuals who consistently meet or exceed expectations in their own tasks. For example, a marketing assistant who is meticulous in managing campaigns is more likely to be trusted when proposing improvements to the team's project management system. Consistency creates a foundation of trust, signaling to colleagues and supervisors that proposed procedural changes are likely to reflect the same level of care and attention to detail.

Effective communication skills also play a significant role in establishing credibility. Being able to articulate ideas clearly, backed by evidence and examples, ensures that suggestions are taken seriously. This involves presenting procedural improvements in a structured, solutions-oriented manner rather than focusing solely on problems. For instance, instead of simply pointing out delays in a supply chain, an employee might propose using specific inventory management software to streamline operations. Additionally, tailoring the language and level of detail to the audience—whether speaking with peers, managers, or executives—demonstrates professionalism and strategic awareness.

Relationship-building is equally essential for establishing credibility. Cultivating trust and respect among colleagues and supervisors creates a supportive environment for procedural contributions. This involves actively listening to others, valuing their input, and collaborating on shared goals. For example, by working closely with team members to implement small, successful changes, an individual can build a track record of collaborative success. Over time, this fosters a network of allies who are more likely to advocate for or implement the contributor's ideas, amplifying their impact.

Credibility is bolstered by taking responsibility for both successes and setbacks. When proposing changes to procedures, contributors must demonstrate accountability for the outcomes. This means being prepared to refine suggestions based on feedback, adapt to unforeseen challenges, and, if necessary, acknowledge mistakes. For example, if a proposed scheduling change leads to unexpected disruptions, owning the issue and working quickly to address it shows integrity and commitment to improvement. This willingness to learn and adapt reinforces the contributor's reliability and builds long-term trust within the organization.

By focusing on these strategies—deep understanding, consistent performance, effective communication, strong relationships, and accountability—individuals can establish themselves as credible contributors to procedural excellence. Credibility is not an inherent trait but a cultivated reputation, built through actions and reinforced over time. With this foundation, employees at any level can inspire confidence in their ideas, making meaningful contributions to their organization's success.

INSPIRATION FOR CHANGE

Driving procedural improvement requires more than technical skill or strategic thinking—it demands a sense of inspiration that ignites change. Individuals who serve as sources of inspiration motivate others to see procedures not as constraints but as opportunities for innovation and growth. Inspiration acts as the catalyst that transforms skepticism into engagement and inertia into action. By fostering a shared vision and leading by example, contributors can inspire change that reverberates throughout an organization.

Inspiration begins with a compelling vision of what could be achieved through improved work procedures. People are more likely to embrace change when they see tangible benefits to themselves, their teams, or the organization. Contributors can paint a vivid picture of how streamlined processes could alleviate workloads, reduce errors, or unlock new opportunities for creativity and collaboration. For instance, a team member advocating for a more efficient project tracking system might highlight how it could save hours of administrative work, allowing more time for high-value tasks. This forward-looking approach generates excitement and optimism, making procedural changes feel less like obligations and more like advancements.

Leading by example is another critical way to inspire change. Actions often resonate more strongly than words, and individuals who model the behaviors they wish to see can effectively influence others. For instance, a team member who proactively adopts and showcases the benefits of a proposed improvement demonstrates its feasibility and value. By embodying a commitment to excellence and adaptability, they set a standard that others naturally want to emulate. This approach also counters resistance, as seeing a peer succeed with new procedures makes them more relatable and achievable.

A powerful element of inspiration lies in highlighting success stories and celebrating small wins. Change often feels daunting, especially when it involves long-standing habits or systems. Sharing examples of past improvements—whether from within the organization or from industry leaders—provides proof that change is possible and worthwhile. For instance, a contributor might share how another department successfully reduced processing time by adopting automation, linking the story to the potential benefits for their team. Celebrating incremental progress, such as smoother collaboration or quicker approvals, helps maintain momentum and fosters a sense of shared achievement.

Empathy also plays a central role in inspiring procedural change. Understanding the challenges, fears, and aspirations of colleagues creates a foundation for trust and motivation. Contributors who take the time to listen and acknowledge concerns can frame changes in ways that resonate personally with their audience. For example, if a proposed shift in workflow addresses a common frustration—such as delays in accessing resources—it can be framed as a solution to that specific pain point. When people feel heard and valued, they are more likely to support and champion the changes being proposed.

Inspiration often stems from a sense of shared purpose. Procedural changes that align with organizational values and goals inspire deeper commitment. Contributors can connect improvements to larger objectives, such as enhancing customer satisfaction, achieving sustainability targets, or fostering innovation. For instance, presenting a new quality control process as a way to ensure customer trust ties the procedural change to a purpose that feels meaningful and essential. This alignment transforms procedural improvements from technical adjustments into contributions to a broader mission, fostering a sense of pride and belonging among those involved.

Inspiring change requires more than advocating for better procedures; it involves igniting the intrinsic motivation that drives individuals and teams to act. By creating a compelling vision, leading by example, celebrating successes, empathizing with challenges, and connecting changes to shared values, contributors can transform procedural improvements into sources of enthusiasm and collaboration. This sense of inspiration not only propels immediate initiatives but also cultivates a culture of continuous improvement, where procedural excellence becomes a shared aspiration.

Skills and mindsets needed to drive change and foster collaboration

Skills and mindsets are the dual engines driving meaningful procedural change and collaboration. While skills provide the tools for action, mindsets shape how individuals approach challenges, perceive opportunities, and interact with others. Together, they form a comprehensive framework for influencing and improving work processes, regardless of one's role or position.

At the heart of procedural excellence lies the ability to navigate complex systems and interpersonal dynamics effectively. This requires not just technical know-how but also a willingness to adapt, empathize, and persist. For instance, a team leader introducing a new workflow system needs both the technical skills to implement the process and the emotional intelligence to address team concerns. Similarly, a frontline worker suggesting improvements to an existing procedure benefits from combining detailed knowledge of the workflow with the confidence and communication skills to present their ideas constructively.

Understanding the interplay between skills and mindsets is particularly vital in collaborative environments. Procedural change is rarely a solitary endeavor—it involves aligning diverse perspectives, balancing competing priorities, and fostering a shared sense of ownership. Individuals equipped with the right skills can articulate their ideas and execute plans effectively, while those with the right mindsets inspire trust, promote inclusivity, and maintain focus amidst setbacks.

This chapter begins by exploring foundational mindsets that underpin successful procedural contributions. These include adaptability, empathy, curiosity, resilience, and a growth orientation. Each mindset represents a lens through which individuals approach their work and relationships, enabling them to navigate challenges with a constructive and forward-thinking attitude.

Subsequently, we will delve into the core skills that translate these mindsets into action. Skills such as active listening, systems thinking, conflict resolution, and facilitation provide the practical tools to drive change and foster collaboration. These capabilities not only enhance individual contributions but also strengthen team dynamics and organizational outcomes. Together, skills and mindsets create a powerful synergy, turning procedural challenges into opportunities for innovation and growth.

By understanding and cultivating these elements, individuals at all levels can position themselves as effective agents of change. Whether leading an initiative, supporting a colleague, or simply offering a fresh perspective, the ability to combine skills with a constructive mindset ensures that contributions are both impactful and enduring. Through the following sections, we will uncover how these attributes can be developed, applied, and integrated into everyday workflows, empowering readers to become champions of procedural excellence.

FOUNDATIONAL MINDSETS FOR CHANGE

Mindsets are the unseen drivers of human behavior, shaping how individuals perceive challenges, interpret feedback, and engage with others. In the realm of procedural change and collaboration, having the right mindsets can mean the difference between resistance and innovation, stagnation and growth. Foundational mindsets enable individuals to navigate the complexities of organizational systems, work across diverse teams, and persist in the face of obstacles. These mindsets are not inherent traits but cultivated perspectives that empower anyone, regardless of their role, to contribute meaningfully to procedural excellence.

Adaptability as a Cornerstone of Progress

The ability to embrace change is fundamental to driving procedural improvement. In a world where industries are rapidly evolving, processes that worked yesterday may no longer be effective today. Adaptability involves remaining open to new ideas, technologies, and workflows, even when they challenge established norms. For example, consider the shift from paper-based systems to digital platforms in organizations. While the transition often encounters resistance, those with an adaptable mindset focus on the benefits—such as increased efficiency and accuracy—rather than the discomfort of change. Adaptable individuals serve as bridges, helping teams transition smoothly and encouraging a culture of continuous improvement.

Curiosity Fuels Innovation

Curiosity is the driving force behind questioning the status quo and seeking better ways to achieve outcomes. A curious mindset leads individuals to ask why processes exist as they do, how they might be optimized, and what innovations could elevate them. For instance, someone working on a manufacturing line might wonder why a specific step takes longer than others, prompting an investigation that identifies bottlenecks and solutions. Organizations that cultivate curiosity among employees often find themselves at the forefront of innovation, as this mindset encourages experimentation, learning, and a willingness to take calculated risks.

Empathy and the Human Element of Change

Procedural change is never purely technical; it impacts people. Empathy, the ability to understand and share the feelings of others, is essential for fostering collaboration and securing buy-in. A manager introducing a new protocol must consider how it will affect employees' daily workflows and morale. By actively listening to concerns and incorporating feedback, empathetic leaders create a sense of inclusion and shared purpose. Empathy also plays a critical role in resolving conflicts and bridging divides between stakeholders with differing priorities, ensuring that procedural changes are both effective and broadly supported.

Resilience in the Face of Setbacks

Procedural change often encounters obstacles: technical issues, resource constraints, or resistance from stakeholders. Resilience—the ability to recover and maintain focus despite setbacks—is a mindset that sustains momentum during challenging times. Resilient individuals view failure not as an endpoint but as a learning opportunity. For instance, a failed pilot of a new process might reveal critical insights that lead to a more successful implementation in the future. This mindset encourages persistence, enabling individuals and teams to navigate uncertainty with confidence.

A Growth-Oriented Perspective

At the core of all effective procedural champions lies a growth mindset—the belief that abilities and systems can be developed through effort and learning. This perspective fosters a proactive approach to challenges, as individuals see them as opportunities for improvement rather than insurmountable barriers. A growth-oriented mindset also nurtures collaboration, as it encourages seeking input from others and valuing diverse perspectives. It empowers individuals to view procedural excellence not as a static goal but as an ongoing journey of refinement and innovation.

By cultivating these foundational mindsets, individuals position themselves as catalysts for positive change. Adaptability ensures they are ready for new challenges, curiosity drives the discovery of innovative solutions, empathy builds strong relationships, resilience sustains progress through difficulties, and a growth-oriented perspective keeps them focused on long-term improvement. Together, these mindsets create a solid foundation for driving procedural excellence, enabling individuals to contribute to organizational success in meaningful and lasting ways.

ESSENTIAL SKILLS FOR COLLABORATION AND CHANGE

While mindsets provide the foundation for approaching procedural change and fostering collaboration, skills translate these perspectives into actionable contributions. Effective collaboration and meaningful change require a combination of technical, interpersonal, and strategic abilities. These skills empower individuals to navigate complexities, align diverse stakeholders, and implement practical solutions that improve workflows and outcomes. Whether contributing from an entry-level position or leading from the top, mastering these essential skills ensures that efforts to enhance processes are both impactful and sustainable.

Active Listening: The Bedrock of Collaboration

At the heart of successful collaboration lies the ability to truly hear and understand others. Active listening goes beyond simply processing words; it involves attentively considering the speaker's intentions, emotions, and perspectives. This skill is particularly crucial in procedural change, where aligning diverse teams often hinges on understanding their unique challenges and contributions. For instance, a process improvement meeting involving multiple departments may uncover conflicting priorities. An active listener can identify common ground by focusing on shared goals while validating the concerns of all parties, fostering trust and a sense of inclusion.

Active listening also creates an environment of psychological safety, where individuals feel valued and encouraged to share their insights. This is essential when introducing procedural changes that might initially seem disruptive. By demonstrating that their input matters, active listeners build stronger relationships, inspire collaboration, and pave the way for smoother transitions.

Systems Thinking: Seeing the Bigger Picture

Procedures rarely exist in isolation; they are interconnected with other workflows, teams, and organizational goals. Systems thinking is the ability to understand these interdependencies and assess how changes in one area might affect the whole. This skill allows individuals to identify unintended consequences, design more integrated solutions, and predict potential challenges before they arise.

For example, a manufacturing team might propose streamlining a specific process to save time, only to realize through systems thinking that the change could create bottlenecks in downstream operations. By mapping out the broader system, they can revise their approach to ensure improvements benefit the entire workflow. Systems thinking enables procedural champions to address root causes rather than symptoms, ensuring that changes are both effective and sustainable.

Communication and Persuasion: Bridging Perspectives

Procedural change often requires navigating differing viewpoints and securing buy-in from stakeholders with varying priorities. Strong communication skills, including the ability to present ideas clearly and persuasively, are vital for aligning these perspectives. This involves not only articulating the benefits of a proposed change but also addressing potential concerns with empathy and evidence.

Effective communicators tailor their approach to their audience, whether it's explaining technical details to specialists or conveying the big picture to executives. For instance, a middle manager advocating for a new reporting system might emphasize its time-saving benefits to employees while highlighting its alignment with strategic goals to leadership. By framing messages in ways that resonate with each group, skilled communicators ensure their proposals are met with understanding and support.

Conflict Resolution: Turning Tension into Opportunity

Change often generates friction, as individuals or groups resist disruptions to familiar routines. Conflict resolution skills enable procedural champions to navigate these tensions constructively, transforming potential roadblocks into opportunities for growth. This involves recognizing the underlying causes of conflict, such as fear of losing control or misaligned priorities, and addressing them through open dialogue and compromise.

For example, two teams might clash over resource allocation during a procedural overhaul. A skilled conflict resolver would facilitate a discussion that allows both sides to voice their concerns, identify shared objectives, and co-create a solution that benefits the organization as a whole. By approaching conflict with patience and objectivity, these individuals foster stronger relationships and a more collaborative culture.

Facilitation: Guiding Teams Toward Consensus

Facilitation is the art of steering group discussions toward productive outcomes, making it an invaluable skill in procedural change initiatives. A skilled facilitator creates a structured yet flexible environment where all participants feel heard, ideas are evaluated objectively, and decisions are made efficiently. This skill is particularly important in workshops, brainstorming sessions, or cross-functional meetings where diverse perspectives need to be synthesized.

Facilitators excel at balancing participation, ensuring that dominant voices don't overshadow quieter contributors while keeping discussions focused on the task at hand. For instance, during a meeting to redesign a customer service process, a facilitator might use tools like mind mapping or voting techniques to prioritize ideas collaboratively. By fostering engagement and clarity, facilitators ensure that teams reach consensus more effectively and with greater commitment.

Critical Thinking: Evaluating and Refining Solutions

Procedural excellence depends on the ability to assess ideas critically, distinguishing between those that offer genuine value and those that might lead to inefficiencies. Critical thinking involves analyzing data, questioning assumptions, and weighing alternatives to arrive at the best possible solution. This skill is particularly important when evaluating the feasibility of proposed changes or identifying opportunities for continuous improvement.

For example, a critical thinker assessing a new software implementation might consider its cost-effectiveness, ease of integration, and potential long-term benefits while seeking feedback from end-users. By applying rigorous analysis, they ensure that decisions are well-informed and aligned with organizational goals.

Building Collaborative Skills for a Better Future

Mastering these essential skills enables individuals to contribute to procedural improvement with precision, creativity, and impact. Active listening fosters trust and inclusion, systems thinking ensures holistic solutions, and strong communication bridges diverse perspectives. Conflict resolution transforms resistance into progress, facilitation drives group effectiveness, and critical thinking ensures that changes are both practical and visionary.

Together, these skills create a robust toolkit for navigating the complexities of collaboration and change. Whether initiating a small process improvement or leading an organizational overhaul, individuals equipped with these capabilities are better prepared to turn challenges into opportunities and foster a culture of continuous growth.

CULTIVATING COLLABORATION THROUGH COMBINED SKILLS AND MINDSETS

The intersection of skills and mindsets forms the heart of successful collaboration and procedural change. While skills are the tools that enable individuals to take action, mindsets shape the attitudes and approaches that guide their application. Together, they create a powerful synergy, fostering environments where collaboration flourishes and transformative change becomes possible. This fusion is particularly critical in procedural contexts, where aligning diverse perspectives and ensuring collective buy-in can determine the success of an initiative.

The Interplay Between Skills and Mindsets

Skills and mindsets do not operate in isolation; rather, they enhance and complement one another. For example, active listening as a skill becomes exponentially more effective when paired with a mindset of empathy. An individual may possess technical expertise in process design, but without a mindset that values inclusivity, their efforts might fail to resonate with stakeholders. Conversely, even the most collaborative mindset needs practical skills like facilitation or conflict resolution to translate intentions into results.

Consider a scenario in which a team is tasked with streamlining a complex workflow. A team member who combines the skill of systems thinking with a mindset of adaptability can better anticipate challenges and propose innovative solutions. Similarly, a manager with strong communication skills and a mindset that values transparency can bridge gaps between departments, ensuring that all voices are heard and integrated into the process. These examples illustrate how the fusion of skills and mindsets elevates individual contributions and strengthens collective efforts.

Creating Collaborative Spaces with Shared Ownership

True collaboration thrives in environments where participants feel a sense of shared ownership over processes and outcomes. This requires both the skills to engage stakeholders effectively and the mindsets to foster mutual respect and trust. Leaders play a pivotal role in creating such spaces, but every team member contributes by demonstrating openness, curiosity, and a commitment to shared goals.

One effective approach is using facilitation techniques that draw on inclusivity and objectivity. For instance, a team redesigning a customer feedback system might hold workshops where participants brainstorm ideas and prioritize changes collectively. The facilitator must combine the skill of managing group dynamics with a mindset that values diverse perspectives. By encouraging participation from all stakeholders, they cultivate a sense of collective responsibility, increasing the likelihood of long-term commitment to the new system.

Balancing Leadership and Collaboration

Collaboration requires striking a delicate balance between leadership and teamwork. Procedural improvement often involves hierarchies, but successful initiatives blur traditional boundaries, allowing individuals at all levels to contribute meaningfully. Skills like critical thinking and communication empower individuals to lead when necessary, while mindsets of humility and mutual respect ensure that leadership does not overshadow collaboration.

Take the example of a cross-departmental initiative to implement a new digital tool. While the IT team might lead the technical aspects, input from end-users is equally critical for ensuring the tool's usability. A project manager with a mindset of inclusivity and the facilitation skills to mediate between technical and non-technical stakeholders can bridge this divide, creating a collaborative environment where all contributions are valued equally. This balance not only enhances the quality of the outcome but also builds stronger relationships among team members.

Overcoming Resistance with Combined Approaches

Resistance to change is a common challenge in procedural initiatives, often stemming from fear of the unknown or perceived loss of autonomy. Overcoming this resistance requires both strategic skills and the right mindset. Conflict resolution skills, paired with an empathetic and patient attitude, are particularly effective in addressing concerns and fostering cooperation.

For example, during the rollout of a new compliance framework, some employees might resist due to increased documentation requirements. A change agent who combines persuasive communication skills with a mindset of understanding can identify the root causes of resistance and address them constructively. They might organize a Q&A session to clarify the framework's purpose, acknowledging employees' frustrations while emphasizing how the changes ultimately benefit the organization. This approach not only eases resistance but also strengthens trust and collaboration.

Sustaining Collaboration Through Continuous Growth

The collaboration fostered by skills and mindsets is not a one-time achievement but an ongoing process. As individuals refine their skills and deepen their mindsets, they contribute to a culture of continuous improvement that sustains long-term success. Teams that prioritize learning and adaptability are better equipped to navigate challenges and embrace opportunities, ensuring that collaboration remains dynamic and effective.

Organizations can support this growth by providing resources for skill development and fostering mindsets through cultural initiatives. For instance, regular training sessions on topics like negotiation or emotional intelligence can sharpen practical abilities, while programs that celebrate diversity and innovation reinforce collaborative values. When individuals and organizations invest in the interplay of skills and mindsets, they lay the foundation for sustained procedural excellence.

The Synergy of Skills and Mindsets in Action

The combination of skills and mindsets transforms how individuals and teams approach collaboration and change. Skills provide the practical capabilities to navigate complexities, while mindsets shape the perspectives that drive constructive engagement. Together, they empower individuals to contribute meaningfully, align diverse stakeholders, and foster environments where procedural improvements thrive.

By cultivating this synergy, organizations and individuals alike can unlock new levels of effectiveness and innovation. In the ever-evolving landscape of work procedures, those who embrace the interplay between skills and mindsets are best positioned to lead with confidence and inspire lasting change.

PRACTICAL APPLICATIONS AND EXERCISES

The true value of integrating skills and mindsets lies in their practical application within real-world scenarios. To bridge the gap between theory and practice, individuals and teams can engage in targeted exercises designed to enhance procedural contributions and foster collaboration. These activities not only build proficiency but also embed the foundational principles of effective change and teamwork into daily workflows. This section explores practical ways to develop and apply the skills and mindsets required for driving procedural improvements.

Simulating Real-World Scenarios

One of the most effective ways to develop procedural competence is through simulated scenarios that mirror workplace challenges. Role-playing exercises allow individuals to practice skills such as communication, negotiation, and conflict resolution while fostering mindsets like empathy and adaptability. For example, a team might simulate a procedural bottleneck, such as a delayed product launch caused by misaligned priorities across departments.

Participants could assume roles like project manager, marketing lead, and technical staff, collaborating to identify root causes and propose actionable solutions. During the exercise, facilitators can provide real-time feedback, emphasizing the interplay between skills (e.g., problem-solving, active listening) and mindsets (e.g., openness to feedback, resilience under pressure). Such simulations encourage participants to approach challenges holistically, preparing them to apply these lessons in actual work settings.

Workshops for Cross-Functional Collaboration

Workshops are invaluable for building procedural fluency across teams and departments. By bringing together diverse stakeholders, these sessions create opportunities to practice collaboration skills while fostering mutual understanding and trust. A workshop on improving a customer feedback process, for instance, might involve representatives from sales, customer service, and product development.

Structured exercises, such as creating process maps or brainstorming potential improvements, can help participants refine analytical and creative thinking skills. Meanwhile, the workshop setting cultivates mindsets like inclusivity and shared ownership. When participants see their contributions integrated into actionable plans, they are more likely to feel invested in the procedural outcomes, ensuring long-term buy-in and engagement.

Feedback-Driven Practice

Feedback loops are essential for refining skills and reinforcing mindsets. Individuals can cultivate feedback as an ongoing exercise, seeking input from colleagues and supervisors on their contributions to procedural initiatives. This practice encourages humility and fosters a growth mindset, allowing participants to view feedback as an opportunity for development rather than criticism.

One practical exercise involves conducting post-mortems or retrospective analyses after significant projects or procedural changes. Teams can analyze what worked, what didn't, and what could be improved, focusing on both individual and collective contributions. Documenting these reflections helps individuals identify patterns in their behaviors and approaches, informing targeted improvements for future initiatives.

Mindfulness and Empathy Exercises

Procedural improvement often requires navigating interpersonal dynamics, making mindfulness and empathy crucial components of collaboration. Practical exercises can help individuals develop these qualities, which in turn enhance their ability to address resistance, manage conflicts, and foster trust.

A simple yet effective exercise involves daily journaling to reflect on interactions and decisions. Participants can note instances where they practiced empathy or responded reactively, evaluating how their mindset influenced outcomes. Similarly, team-building activities like empathy mapping encourage participants to understand stakeholders' perspectives, helping them approach procedural challenges with greater compassion and insight.

Scenario-Based Problem Solving

Problem-solving exercises focused on real or hypothetical scenarios allow individuals to integrate skills and mindsets in dynamic ways. For instance, teams might tackle a challenge like reducing the time required to onboard new employees. Participants can brainstorm solutions, assess potential roadblocks, and outline a revised onboarding process.

Throughout the exercise, facilitators can highlight the importance of balancing technical skills, such as process mapping, with mindsets like patience and creativity. Teams can then implement their solutions on a trial basis, using iterative feedback to refine the process and measure its effectiveness. By combining strategic thinking with emotional intelligence, participants learn to approach procedural improvements as both a science and an art.

Sustained Skill Development Through Practice

Practical application is not a one-time effort but an ongoing commitment to growth. Organizations can support this journey by incorporating skill-building and mindset-reinforcing activities into their regular operations. For example, weekly "procedural improvement hours" can provide dedicated time for individuals and teams to tackle inefficiencies, share ideas, and test new approaches.

In addition, mentorship programs can pair experienced procedural contributors with emerging leaders, creating opportunities for hands-on learning and knowledge transfer. These partnerships reinforce the value of collaboration and continuous improvement, fostering a culture where procedural excellence becomes a shared priority.

Integrating Exercises Into Organizational Culture

The success of practical applications and exercises depends on their integration into daily workflows and organizational culture. When teams prioritize practice and reflection as part of their routines, they build the habits and relationships necessary for sustained procedural success. By emphasizing both skill development and mindset cultivation, organizations empower individuals to drive meaningful change and contribute to a culture of collaboration and innovation.

Through these exercises and their ongoing application, individuals and teams alike can move beyond theoretical understanding, embedding the principles of procedural excellence into every aspect of their work. This hands-on approach ensures that the synergy of skills and mindsets translates into tangible outcomes, creating a lasting impact on both individual and organizational success.

The journey toward fostering collaboration and driving procedural change is as much about cultivating the right mindset as it is about honing practical skills. Together, these elements form a dynamic interplay that empowers individuals to become catalysts for improvement, regardless of their role or organizational context. By emphasizing openness, adaptability, and a collaborative spirit alongside concrete abilities such as effective communication, problem-solving, and process analysis, individuals can transform even the most challenging procedural environments into opportunities for growth and innovation.

As explored throughout this section, the skills and mindsets required to influence change are not innate; they are developed through intentional effort, practice, and reflection. Whether through scenario-based learning, feedback-driven exercises, or cross-functional workshops, the tools for enhancing collaboration are accessible to anyone willing to invest in their personal and professional growth. Furthermore, these practices contribute to a culture of inclusion, trust, and shared purpose, ensuring that procedural advancements are not only efficient but also deeply human-centered.

Transitioning from understanding to application requires commitment, resilience, and vision. While the process may be gradual, the outcomes are transformative—both for individuals striving to make an impact and for organizations seeking to achieve long-term excellence. Embracing this dual focus on mindsets and skills establishes a foundation for sustained procedural success, fostering environments where innovation and collaboration thrive.

In the chapters ahead, we will delve deeper into the nuanced dynamics of procedural influence, exploring how these principles manifest in leadership roles, team settings, and individual contributions. By examining the broader implications of procedural change on organizational culture and personal development, we will uncover how the synergy of skills and mindsets not only drives procedural improvements but also shapes meaningful, lasting progress.

This transition from practical exercises to broader strategic insights marks a pivotal step in understanding the profound potential of work procedures. It invites readers to reflect not only on their own contributions but also on the collective possibilities that emerge when skills, mindsets, and collaboration converge. The journey continues, expanding into how these principles can be leveraged to inspire leadership, navigate complexity, and transform organizations from within.

Turning procedures into a personal and organizational advantage

Procedures are often met with resistance, perceived as restrictive frameworks that limit creativity and enforce monotony. This perspective, while common, overlooks the transformative potential that procedures can offer. Instead of seeing them as constraints, procedures can be reframed as opportunities—tools that provide structure for creativity, consistency, and meaningful contributions. They create a shared language within organizations, allowing diverse teams to align their efforts and focus on achieving common goals. By shifting the narrative around procedures, individuals and organizations can unlock their hidden value.

Essentially, procedures are designed to solve problems. They standardize processes to ensure quality, minimize errors, and optimize outcomes. For individuals, this means less time spent troubleshooting and more time devoted to impactful tasks. A well-crafted procedure liberates rather than confines, offering a clear pathway for navigating complex tasks or decision-making processes. By embracing this mindset, employees can focus on refining their skills and pursuing growth within a stable, reliable framework. Organizations, in turn, benefit from a workforce that understands and values the systems in place, fostering a culture of efficiency and collaboration.

Reframing procedures also involves recognizing their role in innovation. While the word "procedure" might conjure images of rigidity, the reality is that most effective procedures are dynamic and adaptable. They provide the foundation upon which experimentation and improvement can occur. For example, Toyota's lean manufacturing system is based on structured processes that encourage employee feedback and iterative change. This balance between stability and flexibility allows organizations to innovate without losing sight of their goals, proving that procedures and creativity are not mutually exclusive.

Furthermore, viewing procedures as opportunities allows individuals to take ownership of their roles in an organization. Instead of passively following established norms, employees can actively engage with the systems around them, identifying inefficiencies and suggesting improvements. This proactive approach not only enhances the individual's sense of agency but also builds trust and credibility within their teams. When employees contribute to procedural development or refinement, they position themselves as invested stakeholders in the organization's success.

Ultimately, reframing procedures as opportunities requires a mindset shift, one that moves away from viewing them as bureaucratic red tape and toward seeing them as strategic enablers. This perspective fosters a more inclusive and productive workplace, where every team member recognizes their role in maintaining and evolving the systems that support collective success. Through this lens, procedures are no longer obstacles to overcome but tools to embrace—tools that empower individuals and organizations alike to achieve their full potential.

Aligning Personal Goals with Organizational Objectives

In every workplace, individuals bring their own ambitions, aspirations, and unique motivations. At the same time, organizations operate with overarching objectives designed to ensure sustainability, growth, and impact. Bridging the gap between these two forces—personal goals and organizational objectives—is crucial for creating an environment where employees feel fulfilled and valued, and the organization thrives. When alignment is achieved, it not only boosts individual satisfaction but also amplifies collective productivity, innovation, and resilience.

To begin, aligning personal and organizational goals requires transparency and communication. Employees must understand the organization's vision, mission, and strategic priorities to see how their contributions fit within the bigger picture. Leaders play a critical role in fostering this understanding by articulating objectives clearly and consistently. When an individual sees how their role contributes to a company's success, they gain a sense of purpose and significance. For example, a marketing specialist might feel more motivated if they understand that their campaigns directly support the company's expansion into new markets, driving both organizational revenue and opportunities for personal career growth.

This alignment also requires a shift in perspective for the individual. Employees should take time to reflect on how their personal goals—whether professional development, financial stability, or creative fulfillment—can coexist with the organization's needs. For instance, someone looking to enhance their leadership skills might find opportunities to lead projects or mentor colleagues, activities that not only support their growth but also add value to the organization. Viewing the workplace as a partnership, rather than a transactional relationship, helps employees identify areas where personal aspirations and company goals naturally intersect.

From the organizational perspective, leaders must create pathways for personal and professional development within the framework of company objectives. Investing in training programs, mentorship opportunities, and clear career progression plans demonstrates a commitment to employee growth. For example, companies like Google have successfully aligned individual innovation with organizational goals through programs like "20% time," which allows employees to work on personal projects that could benefit the company. Such initiatives empower employees to pursue their interests while contributing meaningfully to organizational success, fostering a culture of mutual investment.

Moreover, fostering alignment involves regular dialogue and feedback. Employees and leaders should engage in ongoing conversations about expectations, performance, and aspirations. This dialogue ensures that personal goals remain relevant to organizational priorities and vice versa. When misalignment arises—for example, if an employee feels their work lacks meaning—it provides an opportunity to recalibrate, identifying new roles, projects, or approaches that restore the connection between individual motivation and organizational purpose. These adjustments keep both parties engaged and committed to a shared vision.

Ultimately, aligning personal goals with organizational objectives is a dynamic and collaborative process. It requires self-awareness, open communication, and a shared commitment to growth. When individuals feel that their personal aspirations are not only acknowledged but actively supported, they bring their best selves to work. Similarly, organizations that prioritize alignment tap into a wellspring of talent, creativity, and loyalty, ensuring long-term success in an increasingly competitive landscape. This synergy transforms work from a series of tasks into a shared journey of achievement and fulfillment.

INNOVATING WITHIN PROCEDURAL FRAMEWORKS

Innovation and procedures are often perceived as opposing forces—one thrives on breaking conventions, while the other relies on maintaining structure. However, this dichotomy is misleading. Effective innovation is rarely about discarding procedures entirely; instead, it involves working within existing frameworks to find creative solutions that drive progress. By embracing procedures as tools for innovation rather than barriers, individuals and organizations can foster environments where new ideas flourish alongside stability and consistency.

Procedures provide a foundation for experimentation. Without them, the chaos of unregulated processes can make meaningful innovation difficult to sustain or scale. Consider the aviation industry, where rigorous procedures ensure safety while allowing space for advancements in technology, fuel efficiency, and passenger experience. In such high-stakes environments, structured frameworks are not the enemy of innovation— they are its enablers. They establish baselines, allowing innovators to identify gaps, inefficiencies, or opportunities for improvement.

To innovate within procedural frameworks, individuals must first adopt a mindset of curiosity and adaptability. Questioning existing processes is not about defiance but about discovery. For instance, a production line worker might notice a redundant step in the assembly process that, if modified, could save time or resources. By leveraging their understanding of the procedure and collaborating with relevant stakeholders, they can propose actionable changes that improve outcomes. These incremental adjustments, often overlooked, are the backbone of sustainable innovation.

Organizations can further support innovation within procedural systems by encouraging a culture of feedback and iteration. Employees at all levels should feel empowered to share observations, propose changes, and test new approaches. Agile project management, for example, is a methodology that thrives on structured iteration, with predefined procedures for evaluating and integrating innovations during development cycles. This balance between adherence to frameworks and flexibility ensures that procedures evolve in response to changing needs, rather than becoming stagnant relics of the past.

Another avenue for innovation is leveraging technology to enhance procedural efficiency. Automation, artificial intelligence, and data analytics can transform traditional processes, enabling faster decision-making, reduced manual effort, and better outcomes. For example, in the logistics industry, procedural innovations like real-time tracking systems have revolutionized supply chain management. Such advancements rely not on abandoning procedures but on reimagining them to align with modern tools and capabilities.

Finally, innovating within procedural frameworks requires leadership that values experimentation and tolerates failure. Leaders set the tone for how procedures are perceived and adapted. By framing them as dynamic tools rather than rigid rules, they encourage employees to think creatively without fear of reprimand. When a proposed innovation doesn't succeed, it should be seen as a learning opportunity, feeding back into the procedural system to make it stronger.

Procedures and innovation are not at odds but are complementary forces. They provide the stability and clarity needed to identify areas for improvement, while innovation breathes life into systems that might otherwise become outdated. By recognizing and embracing this interplay, individuals and organizations can create processes that are not only efficient but also dynamic, adaptive, and forward-thinking. In this way, procedural frameworks become platforms for progress, enabling continuous evolution in a world that demands constant reinvention.

PROCEDURES AS TOOLS FOR LEADERSHIP AND INFLUENCE

Leadership is often associated with charisma, vision, and decision-making, but one of its most underappreciated aspects lies in the effective use of procedures as tools for influence. Far from being mere administrative tasks, well-designed and executed procedures can empower leaders to align teams, drive organizational success, and foster trust among stakeholders. By mastering the art of procedural leadership, individuals can amplify their influence and create a lasting impact on their organizations.

Procedures offer leaders a mechanism to translate vision into action. While strategic goals provide the overarching direction, procedures serve as the actionable steps that bring these goals to life. For example, a company aiming to enhance customer satisfaction may introduce a standard feedback collection process. Through this procedural approach, leaders ensure that every employee—from front-line staff to executives—understands and contributes to the goal. Such alignment not only ensures consistency but also builds a sense of collective ownership among team members.

Leaders who use procedures effectively understand their role in creating clarity and stability within organizations. Clear procedures reduce ambiguity, particularly in times of uncertainty or rapid change. Employees are more likely to trust and follow leaders who provide well-defined pathways to navigate challenges. During the COVID-19 pandemic, for instance, organizations with robust health and safety protocols demonstrated their commitment to employee well-being, reinforcing trust in leadership. By implementing and communicating such procedures transparently, leaders can strengthen their credibility and influence.

Moreover, procedures allow leaders to demonstrate fairness and accountability. A transparent, standardized process ensures that decisions are made equitably, reducing the perception of bias or favoritism. This is particularly important in performance evaluations, promotions, or conflict resolution. When employees see that leaders adhere to established procedures, they are more likely to respect their authority and decisions. In this way, procedures become tools for building an organizational culture rooted in integrity and mutual respect.

Another dimension of procedural leadership lies in fostering collaboration and empowerment. Leaders who involve their teams in designing or refining procedures show that they value collective input. This participatory approach not only improves the quality of the procedures but also increases employee engagement. When individuals feel that their perspectives matter, they are more likely to take ownership of the processes and their outcomes. For example, a manager who invites team members to contribute ideas for streamlining workflows not only gains valuable insights but also strengthens team cohesion and morale.

Procedures also serve as vehicles for influence beyond direct leadership roles. Individuals who master procedural knowledge can wield significant informal authority, regardless of their position in the hierarchy. By understanding and leveraging established processes, they can advocate for change, mobilize resources, and drive initiatives. This influence is particularly valuable in large organizations where navigating bureaucratic systems is essential for progress. For instance, a mid-level employee who knows how to expedite approvals or secure funding for a project becomes an invaluable asset, gaining influence through procedural expertise.

Leaders can use procedures to inspire innovation and continuous improvement. While procedures provide structure, they should not be static. Effective leaders view them as living systems that evolve in response to feedback, technological advancements, and changing organizational needs. By championing this dynamic approach, leaders encourage their teams to challenge the status quo and seek better ways of working. This balance between procedural discipline and adaptability fosters a culture of innovation, ensuring that the organization remains competitive in a rapidly changing environment.

Procedures are far more than operational tools; they are powerful instruments for leadership and influence. By using procedures to provide clarity, ensure fairness, foster collaboration, and drive innovation, leaders can create environments where both individuals and organizations thrive. Whether managing a small team or steering a global enterprise, mastering procedural leadership is an essential skill for anyone looking to leave a meaningful and lasting legacy.

CASE STUDIES AND SUCCESS STORIES

Real-world examples provide compelling evidence of how procedures can be transformed into tools for personal and organizational success. Through case studies and success stories, we can examine how individuals and organizations have leveraged procedural frameworks to achieve remarkable results, inspiring others to adopt similar approaches. These stories highlight the versatility of procedures across industries, roles, and challenges, illustrating their potential to drive innovation, foster collaboration, and enhance outcomes.

One notable example comes from Toyota, a global leader in automotive manufacturing. Toyota's production system, often regarded as the gold standard of procedural efficiency, emphasizes the principles of "kaizen" (continuous improvement) and "just-in-time" manufacturing. By embedding procedures into every aspect of their operations, Toyota revolutionized the automotive industry, reducing waste and increasing productivity. The system's success relied heavily on empowering employees at all levels to identify inefficiencies and propose improvements, demonstrating how procedures can unite personal initiative with organizational goals. This approach not only transformed Toyota's business model but also established a template for other industries to follow.

Another success story involves Mayo Clinic, a healthcare organization renowned for its exceptional patient care. Mayo Clinic implemented standardized care pathways to improve outcomes and ensure consistency across its facilities. These procedures guide physicians and staff through evidence-based practices, reducing variability in treatment and enhancing patient safety. By involving multidisciplinary teams in the creation of these pathways, Mayo Clinic ensured that the procedures were both comprehensive and adaptable to individual patient needs. This case underscores the role of collaboration and innovation in procedural excellence, showcasing how structured frameworks can lead to life-saving results.

On an individual level, consider the story of Sarah, a mid-level manager at a mid-sized technology company. Sarah inherited a team struggling with inefficiencies and low morale due to unclear processes and redundant workflows. By methodically analyzing existing procedures and engaging her team in redesigning them, Sarah introduced a streamlined system that significantly reduced bottlenecks. Within six months, her team's productivity increased by 40%, and employee satisfaction scores rose substantially. Sarah's ability to turn procedural challenges into opportunities for empowerment and efficiency earned her recognition as a leader, paving the way for her promotion to a senior leadership role.

A further illustration comes from NASA's Apollo 13 mission, a case that highlights the life-saving potential of well-designed and flexible procedures. When an oxygen tank exploded onboard the spacecraft, endangering the crew's survival, NASA's ground team relied on established procedural frameworks to develop innovative solutions under immense pressure. The engineers devised a workaround to filter carbon dioxide using materials available to the astronauts, a process that adhered to procedural rigor while accommodating unprecedented circumstances. This success exemplifies how procedures, when paired with creativity and adaptability, can overcome even the most extraordinary challenges.

In smaller-scale settings, freelancers and entrepreneurs often demonstrate how procedures can support scalability and growth. Consider Jane, a freelance graphic designer who struggled with meeting deadlines and managing client expectations. By implementing a simple procedural framework—such as standardized contracts, project timelines, and feedback loops—she transformed her business operations. These procedures not only improved her efficiency but also enhanced her professionalism, leading to an influx of high-profile clients. Jane's story illustrates how even individuals can use procedural discipline to elevate their careers and achieve personal success.

These case studies collectively highlight the transformative power of procedures across diverse contexts. Whether in global corporations, healthcare institutions, or entrepreneurial ventures, they show how procedural frameworks can align goals, inspire innovation, and foster collaboration. By studying these successes, individuals and organizations can draw valuable lessons, adapt best practices, and uncover new ways to leverage procedures for lasting impact.

ACTION PLAN FOR TURNING PROCEDURES INTO ADVANTAGES

Transforming procedures into personal and organizational advantages requires intentional effort, clear strategies, and a commitment to ongoing improvement. An action plan provides a roadmap for individuals and teams to maximize the value of procedures, fostering efficiency, collaboration, and innovation. By following a structured approach, anyone can identify opportunities, implement changes, and measure success.

The first step in the action plan is **conducting a thorough assessment of existing procedures**. Begin by evaluating the effectiveness and relevance of current workflows. Identify pain points, redundancies, and areas of ambiguity that hinder productivity. This phase should involve gathering feedback from those directly impacted by the procedures, as their insights are critical for pinpointing inefficiencies and bottlenecks. Tools such as process maps or flowcharts can help visualize workflows, making it easier to detect gaps and unnecessary complexities. For individuals, this might involve reviewing personal habits or work routines to identify opportunities for streamlining.

The second step is **defining clear objectives for procedural improvements**. These goals should align with both personal ambitions and organizational priorities, ensuring that changes benefit all stakeholders. For example, an organization might aim to reduce lead times by 20% or improve compliance with industry standards, while an individual could focus on enhancing time management or increasing output quality. Clear objectives not only guide the redesign process but also provide measurable benchmarks for evaluating success.

Next, **involve key stakeholders in the redesign process**. Collaboration is essential for creating procedures that are practical, effective, and widely adopted. For organizations, this means engaging employees across levels, from frontline workers to managers, to ensure that the revised procedures address real-world challenges. On an individual level, it might involve seeking advice or feedback from mentors, colleagues, or clients. Collaborative input fosters a sense of ownership and increases the likelihood of long-term adherence to the new processes.

The fourth step is **developing and implementing revised procedures**. This phase requires balancing structure with flexibility, ensuring that the new workflows are adaptable to changing circumstances. For organizations, detailed documentation of the procedures is crucial, including step-by-step instructions, roles, and responsibilities. Training programs or workshops can help familiarize teams with the changes. Individuals might formalize their new routines through checklists, templates, or digital tools designed to support consistent execution. Piloting the revised procedures on a smaller scale can help identify potential issues before full implementation.

Once the new procedures are in place, **establish mechanisms for continuous improvement**. Procedures should never be static; they must evolve to meet emerging needs and challenges. Regularly review the effectiveness of workflows through performance metrics, employee feedback, or self-assessments. Encourage a culture of adaptability where suggestions for improvement are welcomed and acted upon. For individuals, this might involve setting aside time for periodic reflection on personal productivity and making adjustments as needed. Organizations can use feedback loops, surveys, or dedicated process improvement teams to maintain momentum.

Lastly, **communicate and celebrate successes achieved through procedural changes**. Highlighting tangible benefits—such as increased efficiency, reduced errors, or enhanced collaboration—reinforces the value of effective procedures and motivates continued effort. Sharing success stories within an organization can inspire others to adopt similar practices. On an individual level, acknowledging progress and accomplishments fosters confidence and reinforces the commitment to maintaining productive habits.

By following this action plan, both individuals and organizations can transform procedures into powerful tools for growth and success. A methodical approach ensures that improvements are intentional, impactful, and sustainable, turning what might once have been viewed as rigid rules into opportunities for excellence and innovation.

SUSTAINING LONG-TERM ADVANTAGES THROUGH PROCEDURES

The true value of turning procedures into personal and organizational advantages lies not just in their initial implementation but in their ability to deliver long-term benefits. Sustaining these advantages requires consistent effort, a commitment to improvement, and a forward-thinking approach that adapts to changing circumstances. When procedures are treated as living frameworks rather than static rules, they become powerful tools for fostering resilience, growth, and innovation.

To sustain procedural advantages, the first priority is embedding a culture of continuous learning and adaptation. Procedures that evolve in response to feedback and external changes remain relevant and effective over time. This requires organizations to foster an environment where employees feel empowered to suggest improvements and question outdated practices. Individuals, too, must adopt a mindset of curiosity, seeking out new tools, methods, and insights that can enhance their workflows. Regular training sessions, workshops, or reflective exercises ensure that procedural knowledge remains current and impactful.

The second element of sustaining advantages is prioritizing alignment with long-term goals and values. For organizations, this means ensuring that procedures directly support strategic objectives, such as improving customer satisfaction, increasing market competitiveness, or achieving sustainability benchmarks. When employees see how their day-to-day tasks contribute to larger missions, they are more likely to engage with and uphold established workflows. On a personal level, aligning procedures with individual goals—such as career development or work-life balance—ensures sustained commitment and motivation.

Another crucial aspect is maintaining flexibility within procedural frameworks. While consistency is vital, rigidity can hinder innovation and adaptability. Organizations can address this by designing procedures that provide clear guidelines while leaving room for creativity and situational judgment. For instance, workflows might include optional steps for non-standard scenarios or encourage team members to propose alternative approaches when beneficial. Similarly, individuals can integrate flexibility into their routines by setting priorities that allow for unexpected opportunities or challenges.

Sustaining procedural advantages also involves leveraging technology to support and optimize workflows. Digital tools such as automation software, collaborative platforms, and data analytics can enhance procedural efficiency while reducing manual effort. Organizations can invest in systems that provide real-time tracking and feedback, enabling continuous refinement. For individuals, apps that manage tasks, deadlines, or performance metrics can help maintain consistency and identify areas for improvement. Technology not only simplifies adherence but also ensures that procedures remain scalable and adaptable in dynamic environments.

Celebrating the enduring benefits of effective procedures reinforces their value and inspires continued adherence. Recognizing achievements—whether through formal accolades, progress reports, or personal reflection—builds momentum and demonstrates how well-structured workflows contribute to success. Organizations might highlight procedural milestones, such as improved productivity or reduced errors, in company communications. For individuals, taking time to appreciate how streamlined processes have enhanced efficiency or reduced stress fosters a sense of accomplishment and reinforces the benefits of structured habits.

By focusing on these elements, individuals and organizations can sustain the long-term advantages of well-designed procedures. This approach ensures that workflows remain dynamic, relevant, and aligned with evolving goals, turning procedures into enduring assets that drive personal and collective success.

Discover more

Author

Other books

www.ingramcontent.com/pod-product-compliance
Lightning Source LLC
Chambersburg PA
CBHW071023240526
45469CB00006BD/2056